"Tracey-Jane Campbel book. We not only hear wisdom and lessons le and give expression to our voices on-stage and off-stage. TJ does not dodge the issue. Here, as always, it is real, challenging, encouraging and affirming."
– Rev. Davinia Roberts, Baptist Minister

"In this debut offering, Tracey-Jane Campbell reaches out a hand of help like a friend guiding a suffering one through a maze of hurt, fear and trauma of the past. Tracey's words of wisdom forged in the heat of her own experiences, wrap themselves around the hearts and feelings of the reader with comfort and courage to believe that complete freedom and healing can be there. We need more of this in the world. Thank you, Tracey." – Karen Gibson MBE Founder of the Kingdom Choir
"Refreshingly free of psychological jargon and in a clear, open and meaningful way, Tracey-Jane shares her story, life experiences and consequently the impact of the pain from wounds and scars she has suffered. The author sets out a challenge: Wherever you are in life, there is more. To accommodate the more, there must be change. She invites the reader to decide, to believe and work toward freedom, light and love." **– Dr Rache-Rose Burrell, Head of Psychotherapy DTC London**

"With her refreshingly authentic tone, Tracey weaves together a seamless blend of personal experience and history, insight into the human experience, directness with the reader, imaginative writing, and

space and prompts for reflection. Built on the foundations of her own courageous healing process, these pages will offer a unique and treasured source of guidance and sustenance to others seeking restoration themselves." **– Edwin Fawcett, MBACP Psychotherapist**

"Tracey-Jane Campbell invites readers to walk with her as she takes a retrospective journey through some of the places in her life that inflicted physical, psychological and spiritual injuries. This honest and raw account will highlight how possible it is for us all to recover and live 'restored' lives."
– Yolanda Antonio, Psychotherapist and Therapeutic Group Facilitator The Brit School London

I AM
RESTORED

A Companion for the
Healing Journey

Thanks

To the women God sent to me: I love and appreciate you. Thank you for adding such richness to my life. You have been there with love, wisdom, jokes, prayer and encouragement. I would not be where I am without you.

To my mum, your labour was not in vain. I love you.

To Munchie, Pudpud, Pup-Pup and Chicken, the reason for the work, I love you loads.

To my family, I love you.

To my husband, Dave, thank you for holding me accountable whenever I wanted to give up. Thank you for the badgering to get this done! I love you.

My thanks to the team at PublishU for continued support throughout the process.

.

Restored

1. Trapped In a Mind of Grief,

2. No love, no warmth, no peace,

3. Living the lie of life, hiding my silent cries,

4. Facade my face, a lie yet inwardly I die,

5. Tears of defeat, I cry; won't someone see me?

6. I live within a cloud; walk with my head
bowed down,

7. I feel I'm nothing now; won't someone hold me?

8. Searching to find relief; these pleasures
hurting me,

9. My worth I cannot see; won't someone teach me?

10. I live within a cloud; walk with my head
bowed down,

11. But then You were there, telling me that You care,

12. Now I'm restored, my strength, my mind renewed,

And though it seems a dream, how can it be Your
love and grace just given me?

13. Restored, I am restored, and though it seems
a dream,

Oh, how I thank You; I love You, Lord,

14. The person you now see, no longer bound but

free; for Your hand rescued me,
Oh, how I thank You; I love You, Lord,
You came down,
You came down, and now,
I am restored.

Tracey Jane Campbell ©2010

Contents

Introduction

I wake up every morning thanking God that my life is not in my own hands.

We are bombarded with memes and encouragements and motivational speeches that tell us to get on with it, to take our lives into our own hands and win. What does it mean to win, when you feel like you've already lost the battle with yourself? I'm not a believer in sitting down, folding my arms, praying and hoping that everything will just fall into my lap. This for me is somewhat of an abdication of our personal responsibilities towards ourselves and others. What I have learnt, however, is that I can rest in the love of God which gives me the strength to pursue love and wholeness from a position of being held and of being accepted. This really helps me in my most challenging moments.

I can't believe I finally wrote this book. It's been on my heart for years, but it's been left in the back of my mind unwritten. For over twenty years, I have been passionate about women finding their freedom and identity; supporting women in their healing journey, listening, talking and learning from them, writing materials for retreats and workshops, and facilitating safe spaces for women to share and engage with one another. Much of it was sitting together in the shared experiences and recognising the truth of the love of God and the transforming power of grace. I was able to be vulnerable about my own challenges,

I studied and was excited about the things I was learning, and during the process, my life changed. It's a sobering thing to know that you are called to facilitate others in the thing that you so wish you'd had. Often people who have been through abuse or traumatic experiences indeed become caregivers and I realise now that learning this caused me to take pauses to make sure that I was doing what I was supposed to be doing. I even tried deliberately running away from it all – suffice to say that didn't work. My experiences showed me that I was indeed in the right space. This led me to do a theological degree with a pastoral care element, as I assumed that my role would be a traditional pastoral role in the Christian world. However, that was not what God had in mind for me.

It was during a conversation with one of these amazing women years ago that the question of this book came up again. I had said something to her, to which she responded, "Why haven't you shared this stuff in a book yet?" It was one of many times I'd had this question. My chest tightened and all I could think was, "Oh Lord, really?" It's relatively safe to share in small spaces, in conferences, or one-on-one, but the idea of putting down thoughts in a book was like – phew! It was daunting. Well, I finally stopped putting it off, put pen to paper – or rather fingers to keypad – and I began. Yay!

I shared the first draft of the introduction with a friend of mine and he looked at me and said, "I can't hear you in these pages." He essentially said – and I'm paraphrasing – "You have a lot to share, so share it just how you would if someone was sitting right in front of you. Share your heart, share what you've learnt. Don't make an academic exercise out of it but be as free and vulnerable as you are in person. Nobody is marking these pages as a scholarly endeavour." Thanks, Rob! These turned out to be the words I didn't know I so needed to hear. I revisited the pages of this book with my ego duly checked, determined to do just that: to speak to you, the reader, about my own journey of healing and restoration and some of the things I've learnt being on this planet for half a century, such as the pitfalls the crashes and the victories. If you're here reading this book right now, maybe it's just out of curiosity or maybe because you have decided that living with the effects of the damage you have sustained in life, for whatever reason, is no longer an option. Maybe you understand that the cost of avoiding confrontation with your pain is too high and you are so ready to live your life in the freedom, love and grace that you know is possible. Through these pages, I hope to support you on that journey.

This is not a biography. Using the words of "Restored" – a song I wrote upon reflection on my own journey – I delve into some of the themes in the lyrics and have a conversation with you about the experiences. I speak as one who continues to grow in freedom from the effects of childhood and domestic abuse. I am a mother, daughter, teacher, pastoral caregiver and songwriter, who has sung the many cries of my own heart, pleading to be heard, even when I didn't understand my own pain.

Have you ever found it scary to admit that you don't feel hopeful or joyful and that this "love of self" everyone seems to bandy about so freely has seemingly eluded you? Or maybe you feel guilty because the words that flow so easily from you to help others seem to bounce off of you as you continue to struggle with your own self-worth. It is so easy to fill the time. We are so busy with life, that the gaping whole inside of us goes untended until it begins in some way to swallow us up.

The path of restoration and healing can unfold in so many ways. There is no "one size fits all", but there is one truth that fits us all and it is that we are loved, we are already accepted, and we are valuable. You are not alone! I hope that these pages will serve you on that journey and that my words bring inspiration, comfort and a little insight into some of the challenges you are facing. We are objectively healed, restored and free in Christ. It is done. What we have to be brutally honest about without spiritualising it away, is that the acceptance of this truth is hard when our perception of ourselves, the very image of ourselves, has been distorted and marred by negative experiences. You have decided to go on this journey. Yes, it is a decision and a brave one because it launches us into the reorientation of our core outlook, a rewiring of the mind and habits. I choose to call this the journey into love.

At the end of every chapter, I've included a reflection and a blank page entitled, 'The Breath', representing the inhale taken before singing the next line of the song and the breath of God giving us life. We all need to take a breath.

These pages are for your own meandering, to write any thoughts, prayers, or feelings that may come up – whatever you need. It's about you, your journey of restoration – your breath. I believe help comes in the form of community. Our communities of faith, our trusted friends or therapists, books we read and things we listen to, and in the stillness of face-to-face intimacy with our Creator. God created us to live together to exchange our stories and the lessons we have learnt.

So let's do this together.

Tracey-Jane Campbell

YOU ARE WORTH THE ENQUIRY.

"Humans: Complicatedly simple, emboldened cowards, fearlessly fearful, generously stingy, unbiasedly biased, lovingly hateful, beautifully broken, stumbling into standing, unlearning re-learning, vacillatingly focused, sorrowfully funny, peacefully angry, LOVED."

-Tracey-Jane Campbell

Chapter 1

Where Did I Lose Me?

The Oxford Dictionary's definition of grief is an "emotional pain, mental suffering, caused by the death of something or someone, a feeling of great loss." This is part of the reality of life. In some ways, it shows that we are still alive. The capacity to feel the depth of emotional and mental suffering indicates life. It is an indication of love, even though the love might feel absent. It sounds so complex and it is – shock, denial, the feeling of being attacked, sad or overwhelmed. Anger, fear, and anxiety are some of the feelings that a person experiencing grief may encounter. "But nobody died," you'd say. Really?

Isaiah 61:1–3

"To heal the broken-hearted; to comfort those who mourn."

It can be devastating to come to the realisation that you have no idea who you are, what your true likes and dislikes are, what you truly feel, or your style and personality, because for as long as you can remember you have morphed your whole being into whatever shape is most pleasing to those around you. The confusion can overwhelm you as you find yourself constantly saying "yes" when you are screaming "no!" inside. It can cause you to become a chameleon. Our deep wounds tell us we are only lovable or worthy if we deny any inkling of our own needs or desires and are accommodating, even at the expense of our very selves. Somewhere in the distant past, I remember glimmers of a little girl, full of life and vigour; that little one's mind and body were quickly enveloped into things she could not possibly have comprehended. Her life, once full of the lightness of childhood, became full of clouds and shadows, missing chunks of time and reoccurring night terrors. This became her normal.

Maybe for you, the loss of your self-knowledge and identity came much later; the disconnect creeping in slowly over time as the experiences of life eroded your sense of being. Life is a complex thing. Often the things that bring us joy can have another side to them. Family, friendships, school, work – none of these are bad. They can be fulfilling and life-giving, but they equally can become places of torment and trauma as we are impacted by a person or persons in any given space that cause us harm. The wounds are not always easy to recognise and our wounds are not always caused by one cataclysmic event. They can appear as a thousand pinpricks or hundreds of damaging words over time. How our bodies absorb damage is varied. There is no contest about the size or reason for your pain. It can be easy to downplay the things you are experiencing because the world is so full of pain, with so many heartbreaking stories that guilt us into telling ourselves and others that our pain, our experience, is not that bad. A pinprick to one person can be a searing gash for another. Your experience is valid. The way it robbed you of your true sense of self and/or peace is worth taking the time to acknowledge and heal from.

So where did you lose "you"? When did you recognise that you were living a locked-up existence; that the woman you had become was unrecognisable to the woman you yearned to be deep inside, or that you, in fact, have no clue who you even want to be, if you even want to be anything at all? There was a time when I thought that everyone experienced life the way I did. As far as I knew, my life wasn't any different from those around me. It was normal to feel a sense of having two existences – me doing the actions and having the interactions, and the me that was locked up inside watching, trying to pre-empt the responses of those around me, towards me. I walked around in a numb bubble acting the roles I had learnt or had been given. Of course, at the time I was completely unaware of this. This came after reflection; after the light was shined on my dark places and after dissection and acknowledgement. The shadow life is real. Before the realisation dawns on us, everything we experience is normal to us. We know nothing else. Humans can become accustomed to almost anything.

And you lovely one – yes, you! You deserve to be untethered from the effects of the hurt, pain and trauma of a life to which you have been shackled. And, hey, I came here to say you are so loved. Your value and worth are unquestionable and your beauty is unique; to cheer you on through these pages because I know that the voices that tell us the complete opposite are real and powerful. They have been hewn in the fire of repetition, habit, misinformation and lies. They are not easily broken. And this is where the joy comes. We can absolutely be renewed and restored. The fact that we're still here is everything!

Imagine going on a walk and seeing a woman walking around homeless. She is roughly dressed; she is hungry, thirsty and lonely. But she has learnt where she can go and have a wash. She has become accustomed to asking for the bare necessities and taking whatever people choose to give her. She knows how to find shelter. She has become accustomed to this way of life. She is pursued by someone calling her name, pleading with her saying, "You don't have to walk like this. There is a house. That house belongs to you. There are people to take care of your wounds; there are people to dress your scars and to give you new clothing. Everything you need is in that magnificent house and it's already yours." You watch the scene as he tries to hand her the key. She looks at the house and looks at the beauty of it and refuses to take the key because when she looks at herself she doesn't believe she belongs there. You listen as she explains to the man the kind of woman she imagines lives in such a house. She describes a beautiful woman, well put together and her eyes are clear. This woman has no visible scars and she walks with her head held high as she goes in and out of the house. She eats abundantly in the house and she is filled with peace and joy. The man says to the woman, "That woman you're seeing is you. That house is yours. It's just waiting for you to accept it and to step into it." My point is that we can grow so accustomed to living with our pain, our wounds and our issues that we fail to see who we are. We fail to see the beauty of what we have been given because it's obscured. In taking this walk, you have accepted that you are more than the total of all your experiences and that you are looking forward to the woman you are becoming; to the place of freedom that awaits you.

"The joy is your sorrow unmasked. And the self-same well from which your laughter rises was oftentimes filled with your tears." – Kahlil Gibran, 'On Sorrow, The Prophet'

Reflection

Some or all of these statements may not resonate with you, but that's OK. Remember, we're taking time to breathe and make enquiry; to give time and space for the voice of your heart to speak up, to hold up the mirror and look into your own eyes. Some of the enquiries on these pages may bring things up too quickly for you. You may be at a place where you can't answer some questions right now and so have to revisit. That too is OK. Self-awareness is ever-evolving but it is through this often tentative self-enquiry that our awareness arises, our wounds are uncovered and acknowledged and healing can begin.

I know for me, there are questions that I ask myself over and over again and each time the response can vary according to what was happening within me at the time. Be patient and gentle with yourself — it's not a race.

Reflection

Statements to Ponder:

- When everything inside me is screaming, "No, I really don't want to or have the capacity to do this thing asked of me," I say yes because...

- I'm a boss. I get everything done. I feel I have to be able to do everything because...

- I stay in the place of familiarity even if it has become untenable and painful. I tell myself I am content because...

- I am convinced that others' perception of me is the most important thing. I make the effort to put the best outside because...

- I keep myself and my life guarded. I am not intimately acquainted with myself. I show up as different people depending on the circumstance because...

The Breath

It's OK to take the time to get to know me.

Chapter 2
How Do We See?

"No love, no warmth, no peace."

This line in the song seems so intense, even a little exaggerated, like a deep distortion. It was a place of hopelessness where everything looked like it was insurmountable. At one point I was going to change that title because I just thought it was too much. I had to leave it because it was the truth of how I saw life at times. Sometimes the way we perceive our life is uncomfortable and messy. The thought of telling anyone that we know – siblings, parents and friends – that there were times that we experienced feeling unloved, exposed and completely unsettled is a daunting one. We could be deemed delusional or cruel. Our parents would probably be horrified and offended and anyone who did anything nice for us or with whom we shared special moments would undoubtedly be hurt. However, this experience and perspective are not about anyone else; this journey is not necessarily about apportioning blame. Instances of abuse or neglect that undoubtedly impacted us are often, though not always, completely unseen by those closest to us. They shape us in unforeseen ways especially when wrapped up in the love we often feel and expect from those who have treated us this way. I remember when I first realised that the touches I was exposed to were not OK; not the way a child should be touched by an adult.

Somehow the blame and the shame of the encounters became mine.

I mean, why didn't I tell someone? Why did I keep going to that house? I felt powerless. How can the mind of a child even grasp the depth of the power dynamics and manipulation at play in these experiences? The confusion and anger the first time that the hand that usually touched us so gently executed a deft punch, is so much to absorb. Maybe for some of us, the blows were not physical at all but were administered through words; words that spoke to us of our inadequacy and worthlessness or made out that we were unlovable. Maybe there were no words at all, but the silence of secrets and fear, atmospheres in different spaces that had us walking on eggshells and taking responsibility for how the day would unfold. It causes you to fumble around trying to block them out while your world becomes smaller and your mind tries to make sense of the fact that you experience both pleasure and pain at the hands of the same person; that they simultaneously do nice things for you and give you things. Whatever the particular wounds and through whatever set of circumstances they came about, there is no doubt that they have played a part in the shaping of our perspective. The lens through which we view ourselves and our lives has been affected.

How is it possible to be surrounded by people and still feel unloved, alone, and tormented? We are not one-dimensional. The ability of human beings to compartmentalise and be numb and tormented whilst having moments of laughter, learning, and carrying out the daily tasks of life is immense. Two things can be true at one time, just because you had times of laughter and you have some good memories does not make the things you experienced less significant. The way we see is so important. The treatment we have received and the words spoken to us begin to formulate who we know ourselves to be, utter lies that are so deeply rooted in our souls (Let me be clear: By souls, I mean body and mind and every part of us; that they become the truth for us). It may be hard, but in acknowledging these feelings and accepting that our perception of ourselves has been obscured, we can begin to practice compassion for ourselves. So deeply embedded is this way of seeing and experiencing life, that we are often unaware of how much we have been impacted until a situation occurs that uncovers them in some way. This can lead to us having responses that come as a shock to us because they are often disproportionate to the current circumstances we are facing.

When I was in early puberty – very early – I was away at a summer camp (I thoroughly enjoyed them during my childhood). There was a boy who brushed his hand over my chest deliberately. Now he was in the wrong, but my response was to hit him over the head with the side of a tennis racket. I remember being so full of adrenaline and so shaky that my full strength was behind that swing, and I was not what one would call a "lightweight." The racket broke and there was a lot of blood. It has only been recently that I even remembered that episode in my life. But I know now that my response at that moment, though the boy was wrong, was not really a response to what he had done. I didn't have any breasts to speak of. I was responding to the other violations that were occurring in my life at that time. The fear and anger that came over me felt completely out of my control.

Our memories, heart, mind and body are intrinsically linked. We experience every aspect of life as a whole and not in parts, which is why trying to compartmentalise often ends in tears and frustration. Our perception has been built from childhood and though we have heard, very unhelpfully, that "things that happened in the past should be left in the past", or that we should "move on" or "grow up and get over it", the reality is that doing this can be detrimental to us – especially if it means we live a life void of self-examination and awareness, where we deny the reality of the impact our trauma is having on our present experience. We are sentient beings capable of examining, reflecting, learning and changing. For us to wander through life in a state of unconscious existence is so sad. I don't believe we were created to live that way. The habitual ways in which we have been taught by life's experiences to perceive our relationships and surroundings must be challenged in order for us to walk in love and freedom. Isn't it jarring that much of our life experiences only become apparent in hindsight, as we take a look back and see them unravel? Often we're amazed or even ashamed of how oblivious we were to the goings on around us, but there is no need to be ashamed. One of the mysteries of life, is the journey inwards; the getting to know and the unravelling. It's a messy business and not for the faint-hearted, but I can truly say one of the most rewarding things I have ever done is to enter into my inner world by reflection and contemplation. Real life is lived inside out: it's our inner world that transforms our lived experience. It is there that the reality of God with us comes to life and fills, loves and nurtures. Now I'm not saying that the outside world is of no consequence or that we should all escape to a commune where we can insulate and isolate ourselves – although periods like this can be invaluable.

What I am saying is that like many things in life, a greater perspective is often gained with a little distance from an object, environment, circumstance or people. It almost seems like a contradiction looking at our lives from a distance; yet looking more deeply, it is the pulling apart that enables us to be rebuilt or reformed. To be fair, it is often the case that this is the only way it can be done. Who can really see through the blurring tears and confusion of some of the things we experience? Especially if many of the things that happened to you, happened in childhood. As a child you're just beginning your life journey; you're just beginning to understand your environment. Your self-awareness is limited and you are experiencing everything for the first time. As children, if we have experienced good things, then we expect good things. The adults around us are our compass, they tell us who we are and our place in the world. And so we arrive at our teenage years or even adulthood, and somewhere along the line, we begin to sense something is not quite right – perhaps due to the responses we have to certain things that happen around us. You may even have begun to notice that your reactions seem out of balance, or extreme. We start to compare ourselves to others, not because we are particularly self-aware, but because we're hyper-aware of everyone around us; trying to keep ourselves safe and trying not to get hurt. I have come to the realisation that I could not always trust how I reacted to certain things. I didn't always know if it was because I was really in danger if someone felt badly towards me, or if it was my own insecurity and fear of being rejected. I had no compass, no boundary and I walked into situations that caused me more damage, because the way I saw myself and my life was obscured and clouded by the things I had experienced. Our outlook becomes shaped by our pain. One of the questions I practice deliberately asking myself when I'm in different environments – be that personal or professional, familiar or brand new – is, "Through what lens am I looking, feeling and experiencing this circumstance, this environment, this person?" I suppose what I'm saying is that becoming self-aware is an intrinsic part of the healing process.

I want to be present and not detached from myself as I was for so many years. Taking time to ask ourselves this kind of question can help us to be connected in the present moment and maybe notice the things that cause us concern or that we want to work on or change. It's about noticing the thoughts that run through our minds at any given time and the emotions that they illicit. When I came to faith I spent so much time hearing people say different versions of "Don't trust your emotions," "Ignore your emotions," and "Don't listen to them, because they're not the truth." Trying to untangle even that was a minefield.

While I understand what was meant to some extent, I also struggled with that concept because I believe that our emotions are God-given and they are pointers, they are amazing, and they are how we experience myriad things in life. Emotions are not bad: They can indicate what thoughts may be dominating us, and rightfully identifying them can enable us to know where we may have built inappropriate habits. We don't have to let our emotions direct us. But being in touch with oneself and recognising and acknowledging emotions is absolutely necessary. We have to feel them for them to be healed, put in the right place and transformed. We have to be able to give ourselves time to stop and process that. It is in taking the time and care you need, that you can move to viewing and seeing those experiences and those moments in a clear way. I hesitate to say that you will see it in a perfect way, because all of us are so imperfect. However, we can get some clarity and move to the place of seeing where we're present, where we can question and be honest.

Psalm 51:6 speaks of God desiring truth in the innermost parts of us. Isn't that what we want? We want our inner life to be truthful and free, so that we can grow in clarity and understanding; into the peace and love we have been given. Loving ourselves fearlessly comes from opening ourselves up to the love of God, so that we can come to a deep understanding of how amazing He has created us to be. He loves us in all our perceived imperfections because in Him we are perfect. You are loved right now. You don't have to wait for this far-off place of perfection where by some means of great discipline and effort, you have earned the right to be loved. Dare to think about loving yourself.

Reflection

Questions to Ponder:

- When I look into the mirror and observe myself, what do I see?

- Who do I see?

- Can you think of a time that you just felt an absence of love?

- What does "peace" mean to me?

The Breath

I am not perfect and that's OK.

Chapter 3

The Life That Lies and Trauma Built

Hey, lovely one! I hope you are taking deep breaths and I'm so glad you're still here. I believe becoming aware of how we see and how we experience different situations and circumstances is an ever-evolving process and invaluable in our healing. The truth is that this is not always comfortable. A place of self-awareness is the place where we see our ugly side – let's not pretend that it's all beauty and greatness around 'ere! When we see our less desirable traits, it can prove quite alarming. I know I've bumped into myself a few times and thought, "Oh my days! I can't believe I thought that or I felt that towards this thing or person." If we are going to really grow into love, then we must embrace ourselves in our entirety. Hiding from ourselves only keeps us from the transformation we so desire. I know I'm not alone, every single person on the planet has their ugly.

There is such freedom in being able to look in the mirror and say, "This is not the best representation of me. That's not the person I want to be." That's OK. It's OK to acknowledge the parts of us that we desire to be different. Now, I want to be really clear right now – I am not talking about physical traits. I'm talking about the lies we believe; the very things that become the building blocks for our lives and eventually shape the life we live. I often think about how the lies we absorb can be twofold – the exaggeration of our innate goodness or the exaggeration of our innate badness. I think that both of these extremes can be harmful to us: the things we desire and wish for other people, the traits that we have denied or failed to see, the ways we have convinced ourselves that we are really good people, nice, empathetic and always really loving. This all makes us feel better about how we show up in the world and it makes us feel that we have nothing in common with those who have hurt us. Conversely, we are unlovable, unclean and have something to be ashamed of; we are so worthless that we must be careful about revealing ourselves to anybody. Because if we are stupid enough to trust people, we deserve anything that happens to us. We built the person that we needed to survive to insulate ourselves. We didn't know that the life we were building could become a cave, where we would scream wildly, unheard, a fortress so well constructed out of broken pieces that it would eventually have to be taken apart and reformed piece by piece.

I remember being thoroughly convinced that I knew my own mind; that I was making my own choices and that I was an independent thinker. Some people might say I was wrong and strong. Now as I look back, yes some of my choices – a lot, actually – were detrimental. However, in my mind, at the time, I was so sure that the decisions were my free choice. I had no idea that my pain was making my choices for me.

That showed up in different ways: being "lacklustre" and not doing my best at something I thrived at because of my need to avoid being singled out as different. You can convince yourself that you no longer desire to do a thing, and actually believe the lie you're telling yourself. It can look like self-sabotage and it can look like hurting someone before they hurt you, because of course they inevitably will hurt you. I mean let's be honest, if we're looking back at the teenage years, the normal hormonal transitioning of that time of life is already massively overwhelming and challenging: We just want to belong. This along with wounds we carry in our bodies that we don't really understand, brings even more complexity. For me this resulted in the formation of, let's call it the "pretend hard shell." Nothing could get to me; I was just fine. Nobody would ever know that there was anything wrong with me. I was laugh out loud, ebullient and outspoken in my persona – ring any bells? Every school report had some version of "Work is good. Would be better if she didn't talk so much in class." I didn't want anyone to see me as too studious, so I joined in with the disruption. The lie that I believed came from having no intrinsic sense of my value and worth. The pain of feeling less-than caused me to believe that I was just doing what everybody else did and I was choosing to do that. I was wearing somebody else's clothes for much of my life; wearing a whole suit of clothes that didn't fit because somewhere deep inside, I felt inadequate and like I had to be accepted by a particular group of people. Life showed me I was only worth so much and somehow it was easier than to accept that I had other desires that I didn't believe I was good enough for.

I enjoyed so many aspects of growing up: My teenage years were both scary, painful and a lot of fun. We know when something doesn't feel safe or is no longer fun. When we retreat, the feeling comes of retreating into ourselves and separating ourselves from what's going on around us, or from what's being done to us – being there and yet absent. You are carving yourself up into different parts while trying to hide your shame, fear and needs. So you get "aggy", "armoured up" and "impregnable" (at least you try to do that but it doesn't really work). You walk around with the constant fear of being exposed as a fraud, of people knowing that you just want to feel safe and loved for who you really are. You're not quite sure who that is, it's not who you are portraying, but that's all you have.

Every so often somebody sees your vulnerability, somebody spies it out, and if it's not a person who is caring, it's worse still if they are dealing with their unresolved trauma and it can be devastating. Especially if you believed they cared about you, only to find they want to break down and destroy the armour you've built in order to cause you further wounds. If that has happened to you, it was not your fault and no, you didn't deserve it. Maybe you were the one who hurt someone with your words or hurt somebody because you could not risk being vulnerable. Such a process is also one of learning to forgive yourself. Are you in some way going to dismantle the life you've built during this process?

Yes, I believe so. There is a restructuring and a dismantling, yeah. But it is as beautiful as it is hard.

You don't have to keep the life you have built. You are under no obligation to continue to live in a way that is not wholesome healthful and freeing for you. It's OK to change your mind. Any voice that doesn't say about you what God says about you is a lie, even if that voice is your own. We are made in the image of God, beloved by and precious to Him. He's not angry at us. He doesn't see us as worms, contrary to too much popular theology and some well-beloved hymns. In our humanity, we experience life in this world, with all its harshness, pain, beauty and contradictions. Humans are beautiful and cruel and I'm so glad that there is a truth into which one can immerse oneself that is bigger than any lie that we've ever believed.

Reflection

Questions to Ponder:

- What are the lies I believe about myself?

- Do they still serve me?

- What place in my life is still protected by the building blocks of brokenness?

The Breath

It's OK to change my mind. It is God's desire that I rest in His love, peace and truth. Lord, I thank You. I choose to be free from the lies that trauma built and as I take this journey with You, I thank You for the wisdom and comfort of the Holy Spirit and I thank You that You are always with me.

1 John 3:1

Chapter 4

Lies and More Lies

What's a facade? The Oxford definition reads as follows, "The front of a building: the way somebody/something appears to be which is different from the way somebody/something really is."

So here it is – this grand feat of technology, one of those new builds that look wonderful on the outside. It's the layer of concrete, metal or wooden layer on the outside coupled with the large modern windows that make it look wonderful. You walk into the new lobby and see the shiny fixtures and fittings, the new shiny lift and the fresh carpet. As you exit the lift to the apartments, you get a closer look at the plasterboard walls and suddenly the materials that seemed so plush no longer look so sturdy. You realise as you move in your furniture, that the places where the walls have been bumped actually have holes in them, and the layer of paint is not as thick as you imagined. You can hear every conversation, cough and bodily expulsion from the units around you. Outside it looks great, but you know that in a short space of time, that place is going to start to fall to pieces if you don't keep up the facade. We are masters at facades: it's very natural and even necessary for social cohesion to have ways of being in different settings. Every society has its social "norms." This is not necessarily a negative thing; just a way of human interaction. If we're going to certain places or events, there may be a dress code or a certain etiquette often unwritten. Cultures often have different social norms and that's why we need to be aware of certain customs (for instance, when we travel to different countries). For the most part, we're aware of this. We grew up with them and we adhere to many of these things automatically for career advancement or acceptance within a group or maybe just in order to stay hidden. There is a limit to some of these norms, depending on when they were set, why they were set and by whom. We have them in churches. Anybody who has visited a church knows that different denominations have their norms. Step outside of those, and you might experience being misconstrued, perceived as not holy enough, not spiritual enough, mature enough, etc. Church communities also develop a culture and it's not always about being "biblical," but about being human. So let's talk about masking: we all do it to some degree or another.

I realised pretty early on how easy it was to put on a mask and project an image of well-being to those around me. Often it's a matter of survival. We are guarded. We don't know who we can trust with the reality of what's going on inside of us. The conflicts we have, the insecurities we have: If they saw the ugly thoughts that sometimes roll through our minds, how would they handle it? We don't know. The fear of rejection or fear of reprisal keep us locked up in our silence; slowly withering inside. We don't want to be the outcast. Our feelings scream at us that we would be the pariah of the playground, of our church, of our college, or our community. And so we allow ourselves to put on the faces that fit; faces that we believe project the image of success and complete control and keep us safe.

Please don't feel condemned or judged by this. Do you recognise this mask in your life? This was definitely true in my life: The smile that was often plastered on my face was self-preservation. It was the look of contentment I wore to avoid conflict in the home; to make sure that "peace" would be kept. I felt like I was literally preserving my life and holding myself together by a thread. I had so many conversations with God asking how someone could sit in a crowd of people and speak, smile and laugh while a completely different dialogue was going on in their minds. I did that with my chest feeling like it would implode under the weight I felt – tears just a blink away and everyone seemingly oblivious. Have you seen her, that woman, who can't face going home, so she stays out as long as possible, taking part in group activities, because she must have witnesses, evidence must be available, proof of where she has been? Have you ever been her? It can be so hard to find places of safety in a world so full of projections of success and perfection. Among "spirit-filled", triumphant people it's understandable to feel like nobody else is going through what you're going through. Intellectually we know there are others and still asking for help can be one of the hardest things. Lies are so powerful – we look around us every day and see these headlines and politics everywhere. Wherever we look, we see lies. Deception is a massive thing and plays a bigger role in our journey than we could ever imagine. We have been deceived.

There is a real battle; the battle to keep us shrouded in the lie of our unworthiness our inability to heal, and ultimately keep us disconnected from ourselves and our true source of love. But you don't have to be disconnected, because that source of love is with you right now where you are, at this very moment. Remember that pasted smile? I discovered that it was not a complete lie. In all my tearful questioning, I've never received a neat compact answer. The lie I believe we've been sold, is that we should expect life to fall into neat compartments and so far I've discovered that it rarely does. We need each other and our realities co-inside by design. A smile can hide so much pain, bring joy to others and simultaneously have a positive effect on us. Turns out that there have been numerous studies on smiling, and overall they have shown that smiling, even when you don't feel happy and just decide to smile, positively affects the brain, lifting your mood, and heart rate, and helping alleviate stress; they are even contagious.[1] I am not suggesting for a moment that we ignore what's going on inside us and just keep smiling. However, what I am saying is that I believe those times of being around others and smiling, even though it felt forced, helped me get through some of the toughest times. We can be suffering, in pain and turmoil and still have happy moments. Be gentle with yourself. You are not a fraud. You are a person on the road to discovery; beautifully human.

Reflection

Statements To Ponder:

- I am conscious of wearing a mask in certain environments. When I do, it makes me feel...

- I don't recognise any times of wearing a mask. I never really thought about it.

The Breath

I'm learning to listen inwardly. I don't ignore my feelings, but I realise that joy can still show up in my hard places.

Psalm 139:14

Chapter 5

God is Not Tired of Your Tears

Nothing has marked my healing journey more than tears – so many tears. Oh my gosh, I was so fed up with crying. I had a season where I would constantly find myself at the front of church services to receive prayer over and over again. The tears also seemed to be unending. I say "season" because of a clear passage of time. When I look back, it really felt like years and years of unravelling. I felt like nothing was coming together and the more I got to know myself, the more pain I discovered. I was tired of myself and so I felt that God must be tired of me too. My tears felt like a defeat. They felt like a failure in some part because many, I believe, well-intentioned people showed their own discomfort over my tears, and that accusatory voice inside me would whisper, "You're taking too long to get the hang of this. You are a person of faith. You should have been over this by now." Have you ever felt like this? If you have ever felt fed up and exhausted by the number of tears you shed or that God was tired of your tears, I'm here to tell you that nothing could be further from the truth: The Lord is not tired of your tears. The lover of your soul is not saying, "Hurry up and get over it." That is not God's posture towards us. Jesus has stepped into your pain, He walks with you in it and through it, and He shares the pain of all your infirm places. In the early years of my faith walk, every time I would lead worship there'd be tears (that really hasn't changed that much, but anyway). One day after a particular service an older lady came up to me and said, "Don't worry. It's just immaturity. When you're mature, you won't cry so much." I could never have imagined at that moment how damaging that simple sentence was to me. It took me a really long time to realise that it was a projection: her understanding of what "being mature" in the faith meant. That simple sentence kept me stuck for a long time. I tried to suppress the tears and thought there was something wrong; that I had so much maturing to do to stem the flow of tears when, in reality, it was me connecting to God and God at work in me.

It was some time afterwards, while leading worship in the same church, that another older woman came to me crying and said, "Your tears really ministered to me." The release and vindication I felt were indescribable. It was as if, in an instant, I was shifted from one place to another. I felt seen. I knew that my prayers, my tears and my questions had been heard. The first lady who spoke to me was doing so from her own experience, and that is what we do as human beings. We are flawed. Even with the best intentions, sometimes we can hinder or hurt someone without knowledge. How many times have you been in a situation where you've been overwhelmed by tears and you couldn't really understand all the reasons why? It's so easy to castigate ourselves and to think that we should have gotten over stuff because of the years that have gone by. However, if these things are not examined and if we haven't learnt how to care for and consider ourselves, we can become stuck; berating our so-called immaturity or perceived lack of faith. God understands our tears. There are multiple reasons for this. Tears can come from being overly stressed or anxious; from deep wounds that are buried and can find no other outlet. Tears can come from shame, from that nagging feeling of not being good enough. They can be an expression of joy, love, relief, anger and fear. They are a gift we've been given; a release for our bodies. They can be a mystery. We don't seem to like mysteries. We like everything sewn up in nice, neat boxes. We are supernatural and we believe in the supernatural God. Therefore, we must leave room for the mystery of knowing that the Holy Spirit is at work in us, together with us. So what about those gut-wrenching tears that show up at inexplicable moments? What about when you feel that others around you are moving but the emptiness and the darkness you feel will not move away? You cannot see a way to go and it feels like a place you will always be. I know it's hard and sometimes words fail us. We have to try not to assume anything about where anyone else is, because the truth is, we don't know most of the time how people are really doing.

Human beings can be incredibly dismissive of tears. It can be really uncomfortable for us. It's not necessarily a lack of care; the tears of others can bring out people's stuff. Tears have been weaponised to cause people damage. They've been used to exaggerate pain and to cause people to get into serious trouble. Tears communicate so many things that I think people worry about; trying to understand what is being said when they flow. When it seems we have been crying for years or been stuck in the presence of the same people, our own shame can cause us to imagine that they're frustrated with us. We have to look at this another way. Sometimes there is frustration, but have you ever thought, rather than being frustrated with yourself, that there are some people frustrated for you because they so desperately want to help and don't know how? Sometimes, because we see ourselves as insignificant, it's easy to assume bad intent from others towards ourselves. We hate to think of ourselves as a bother to anyone and yet we want to be seen and heard. We want to know that our pain matters to somebody. I want to know that my pain matters to God. Psalm 56:8 speaks of our tears being recorded by God. This always spoke to me of care and understanding, letting us know that we are not overlooked. I spent a lot of time in the Psalms in my most painful moments. In it, I found some language to express what I was feeling and some language for my prayers.

The secret tears you cried in your bed at night, in communal moments, or even during a counselling session, were not unseen. You are not unseen. It can be hard to believe this when we don't see anything changing; so incredibly defeating when we don't feel love. We feel unseen because in some ways we are still hiding from ourselves and so remain hidden from the majority of people around us. This is a catch twenty-two situation. How can we take the risk? The world can be harsh. If people do treat us badly, we are quite capable of internalising this treatment as confirmation of the wrong ideas we hold about our value. And so we perpetuate a cycle. We hide and then we're not seen or we feel we are not seen.

The place of our pain is tender when it remains unhealed. It's like a fresh bruise – it hurts when touched. I used to find myself crying when I couldn't express myself with words, full of tears of rage at any kind of confrontation or falling to pieces when I felt incapable of completing a task. I didn't have the tools to stand up for myself, to tell people what I needed, or to set safe boundaries. I had to permit myself to learn. As you take your time in your process, you will learn that your needs are important, you will grow in understanding how things show up for you in your body and emotions and you will learn to trust yourself more. Even as I type this I hear in my mind, "Lean not on your own understanding." That was so drummed into me, but not in a helpful way. Rather than an instruction to trust in God, to lean on His love for us and His direction, I understood it in a way that seemed to discourage asking questions and developing critical thinking.

Fortunately, I was inquisitive enough to ignore those wrongly interpreted instructions. I am so grateful to God that He meets me every step of the way with every inquiry and gives me peace to trust in the mystery. Trust me, you have been seen by people whom you don't expect; people praying for you that you have no idea about. Psalm 84:5-7 is one of my favourite Psalms. I found it at a time when I was exhausted with tears. It says,

"Blessed are those whose strength is in You, whose hearts are set on pilgrimage. As they pass through the Valley of Baka ("tears"), they make it a place of springs; the autumn rains also cover it with pools. They go from strength to strength, till each appears before God in Zion."

Right now you might not feel that your tears will bring you to pleasant places of freedom and joy. The thing that brought comfort to me in this Psalm is that the people were walking through the valley of tears. They were not pitching a tent there. Those tears form into springs of life. There are a lot of illustrations of journeys in the scriptures, because that's what life is. The love of God is yours right now. With every step you take forward, no matter how small, you grow into strength and freedom as your loved, healed, joy-filled self is revealed. Imagine this change and expect it.

You are amazing. Just remember the number of times you got on with life, took care of your responsibilities, cared for others and laughed when you felt like crying (not necessarily out of obligation but because you wanted to). You gave what you so desperately needed to receive, you gave out of your own pain to people who were experiencing things you recognised. You carried others even when you so needed to be carried. It's OK to take the time to nurture yourself and nurture your own heart. Put yourself in your schedule.

You are on the road to acknowledging your whole

self, to accepting the best parts and the worst parts of you. Accepting our flaws doesn't mean we don't want to change and doesn't mean we think all the ways we think and behave are OK; but, unless we accept that we have weaknesses and strengths, positive and negative thoughts and behaviour, it's much more difficult to move forward. You are loved by God in your entirety and so you must accept yourself in your entirety – every crevice and corner of your beautiful, challenging self. Then you can look at this self with honest eyes and open her up to the truth of love. We have to know that if we don't accept ourselves fully, it's very difficult to find others who will. We will forever contort ourselves to fit into places that we want to be to gain acceptance. Unfortunately one of the easiest places to hide is behind religious language, because living a life of faith, hope and belief can be so easily conflated with living in deception and living in denial. Believing that our healing and wholeness have already been accomplished for us – which I do believe – can make us feel that we don't have a role to play in the shaping of our own life experiences. If it's already done, if the work for my healing and freedom has already been done, then I just have to kind of wait to experience it, don't I?

If I discuss some experiences that seem contrary to all these wonderful promises, am I in danger of denying my faith? Well, no. I'm telling you, I have been in a place where I have spoken and spoken these truths and it has kept me strong and allowed me to see some unbelievably powerful things – yes, I

53

believe in miracles. However, it has also kept me from seeking help for a long time, because I thought that if I went for help if I went to research the effects of abuse or how to deal with being depressed, then I was somehow not a person of faith. I think we give the world and the enemy way too much power. It isn't knowledge, but the lack of it that makes us perish. It's what we do with the knowledge we have that matters. We are one with the Creator of the universe, so I look at this process as something we do with God, it's one way that who we really are is revealed to US: God already knows.

This is a journey where the effects of one Kingdom are revealed and transformed by immersion into another; it's a journey of the transformation of the mind. We trust, we pray, but we also get our hands to work, and get help from those that we can learn from. So I choose to say: I am healed and being healed; I am restored and being restored. This is quite theological language but I've thought about it a lot and for me, it's the best way to describe what I believe about walking out the healing journey. The Kingdom of God is now and is to come – both statements are true. The language of faith is, "both, and"; not "either, or". It is a mystery, it is wisdom and faith: I believe we need all of these. Wise counsel comes in many forms, and you may be fortunate enough to have a circle of people that you can confide in. I know that there were many days I would not have survived without the listening ear of a few beautiful and powerful friends who held my pain in confidence. There are amazing resources and books that we can learn from. For me, books were my best friends throughout many transitions. Seeking professional therapy doesn't make you less of a person of faith and it doesn't make you less spiritual. In fact, I think it is an indicator of self-awareness. It's a good thing when you know that you need support to help work through and navigate your wounds and tools to change some of your learnt habits and ways of thinking. From gathering in our communities and prayer groups to coaches, physical exercise and mentors: we have choices. My point is that no two journeys to healing and restoration are the same. Things that help us at different times can change and that's OK.

Reflection

People often see what we want them to see. Take a minute to think about the person you present to the world. Who is she?

Statements To Ponder:

- I cry a lot and I often don't know why...

- I don't cry that much. I often feel like crying, but I hold my tears...

- I'd rather work through my trauma alone with God...

The Breath

I am seen by God even when I feel unseen. My tears are not too much. My tears will bring me to a stream of flourishing. Through the tears, I will move forward and I will grow stronger as I know how much I am loved, and I grow in love with myself.

Chapter 6

In the Grey Depression and Its Many Faces

The Mayo Clinic describes depression as "a mood disorder that causes a persistent feeling of sadness and loss of interest (hopelessness), also called 'clinical depression'. It affects how you feel, think and behave and can lead to a variety of emotional and physical problems."

Depression is a big subject and quite an intimidating one. It took me a long time to accept that what I had labelled "the cloud" for so many years was in actual fact depression. There are far more people speaking openly about it now than we ever had twenty years ago. Sure, that's due to the development of social media. I definitely think that's a good thing. My peers were very reluctant to label their down days or feeling a bit more sad than usual, depression. I definitely was. I had an incomplete understanding of it. When I thought of depression, it was clinical depression where people took medication and were not able to function. I never understood all the different nuances, so anything I was facing seemed minuscule in comparison. I didn't realise that I had experienced depression until I started to emerge from the other side of it and took the time to look into it and do some work.

Most of us by now have heard people talking about depression quite flippantly with phrases like "everybody has down days" and "get up and brush yourself off. Think positively." Sadly, I have been guilty of that myself. It's true that just because we experience days of feeling down or irritable, it doesn't necessarily mean we are depressed. We all have mood swings. Depression has many faces and different depths. The symptoms are definitely not a one-size-fits-all. The discovery that someone could be in full-blown depression and still be laughing and smiling was a relief to me. It was a relief to know that the action of going through life laughing and interacting with people, whilst having this cloud was actually a real thing. It gave me clarity about my own experience. I remember those days vividly – it was like seeing life through a sepia filter. Nothing had its full vibrant colour. However, I wasn't aware that this was depression. I had no reference for depression. There was no awareness that my inability to enjoy anything could be linked to depression. On the outside, I appeared confident; "the life and soul of the party." But I remember how it was to get home after interacting with everyone, unnaturally exhausted. It was as if there was this whole person that I removed and put on again to face life. It's difficult to explain the cloud. I would wake up every morning as if I had hooded eyes. There was white behind my eyes and heaviness in my chest. The second after I woke the cloud would descend. It wasn't even a sad emotion; it was more like nothingness. And so I would put on my costume and try to find ways to have the fulfilment that I felt everyone else was having – at least on the days when I left my house. The cloud walks with you and you're never free of it. I know I've gotten a bit metaphorical, but it's the only way that I can really describe the experience. It wasn't just a mental experience but a very physical one in the sense that I also felt the heaviness in my body (and no, I don't mean the excess weight!). I've had this experience at least twice in my life: in my teens and as a young parent. Thankfully, I didn't experience it to the point where I couldn't function at all, but I definitely had times when I was barely getting by.

What did I do? I muddled through. I had the responsibilities that life brings and I didn't have time to stop. Often I would pray and cry, sometimes I would sit and stare at the wall and want to disappear. I couldn't be depressed, because sometimes I'd laugh and genuinely find something funny. I would have powerful times in the presence of God, alone and leading worship, feeling real relief, peace and love in those moments. It sounds contradictory, doesn't it? This is one of the reasons I knew that I had to write this book. Although it has been in my heart for many years, now was the right time because I am free from so many of the damaging ways I used to think, both about myself and about God. If you are experiencing any of this, I want you to know that it's not a contradiction. It was my encounters with Jesus that kept me and assured me through these times, and He will keep you, He's with you and He won't leave you in the middle of your struggle. He's not angry with you.

What do you do when your tentative questions and probing result in pat answers like, "The joy of the Lord is your strength"? I knew that it was God's joy and grace that was holding me together and still I would self-medicate (I will speak more about that later). Your mind is bombarded with thoughts that if you're praying enough or if you're reading enough scriptures you wouldn't have these things, and then you look at your life and feel like a failure because you are experiencing this weight and no matter how many tears you shed, it doesn't seem to get any lighter. What do you do with that? Where do you go?

I remember sharing my experience of domestic abuse with a cousin of mine years after the fact and he was absolutely horrified. His actual response was, "I never saw you as a person that could experience a thing like that, because you seem so strong and so vibrant." Man, I was so good at hiding. I think I was aware that I was seen that way and I'm sure it played into my need to present that to protect myself. It was the shame of seeming weak and the shame of imagining people's perception of me being diminished in some way. The fear of shame is such a crippling thing and sadly this is especially true if you are in the faith community. Yes, we are in the twenty-twenties (or twenty twenty-four) and one would think that this was not the case any more. Things have changed a little. Many more things are being done about mental health care and much more is being discussed; yet the gap in the understanding of the importance of mental health care and the actual action of providing care or signposting to places of support, is still woefully large. There is a shame that comes with being in a faith community and feeling like you should be handling everything and like your spiritual life is not up to par if you are dealing with any kind of mental health issues. Believe me, I've heard the whispers in bathrooms when people don't know you're there, the comments passed in green rooms when someone's life seems to be "out of order." I've sat down and engaged in too many of those conversations when I should've left. For many years now my standard response to any kind of storytelling has been, "I don't want to know." I don't want to hear what "a little bird told you." I don't want to hear what anybody "pinched and told you" (an old Jamaican saying we used to hear a lot in church). I had to learn to become the safe space that I also wanted to have.

As women, we have been, and continue to be, fed this rhetoric of a strong woman and what it means to be a "Proverbs 31" woman. In my opinion, the Proverbs 31 woman has been used quite abusively, becoming the bane of many women's existence. The superwoman model has a career, she takes care of everything in the household, she upholds her husband, probably boasting of his prowess, she does charity work and she does all of this whilst, in a blissful state of deep spiritual connection, authority and wisdom, she's a prayer warrior who can carry anything, do everything with a stiff upper lip without wavering and seemingly without any help (at least, that's the way the image has been sold to us). We don't see what her husband does except to be honoured at the city gate and feel proud. We women are amazing but what life has taught me, through observation and listening, is that many women just suffer in silence. They suffer with their battles and with the pain in their hearts. They pray, they trust and believe God and they don't want to feel ungrateful. They don't want to be perceived as lacking in faith and they definitely do not want to be seen as unspiritual. So they sit with "the cloud" and this often shows up in their physical and mental health later in life. Please don't try to be "Superwoman." You may hold the Proverbs 31 woman up as your ideal if you so choose, but know, she is not a real woman. She's an "ideal" picture. I'm going to refrain from getting into a discussion about why King Lemuel's mother might paint such a picture for her son. That's for another time. You are a real woman with real feelings and needs; don't abandon yourself.[2]

When the line from my song, "Walk with my head bowed down" came to me, I thought about what that really meant to me. Walking with your head bowed down is a false humility. In this instance, if the head is bowed down, it is saying, "I am not worthy." It is saying, "I am getting by, doing what I can, barely making it, but I never complain." The woman with the bowed head never asks for help, because she feels unworthy of anybody's time, and doesn't even know where is a safe place to ask. Yet her posture screams silently, "Someone, see me!" For the most part, the posture is not external: It's a folding up on the inside, while externally she could be throwing herself into trying to have fun and even coming across to some as proud and confident. Rarely do people have access to every part of another human being. If you have really strong intimate friendships with people that you can be candid with, warts and all, you are blessed. These relationships are sadly few and far in between and they should be treasured. So many people are just trying to do the journey alone, until they get a bit more fixed, clean and in order. That's what the Gospel is for: It's not your job to clean yourself up. It's your gift to walk with God into freedom and let Him show you who you are in Him and how to take care of yourself. God is ordering your steps and He will guide you where to go for help.

It's not OK for you to feel you have to sit with these experiences alone without anyone to speak to. How is your sleep? Are you experiencing anxiety, feeling restless and agitated? Do you feel like you can't remember the last time you felt any pleasure or even felt anything? Are you really lethargic or having suicidal thoughts? All of these things could indicate some form of depression. I am aware that so many other things can cause these kinds of symptoms. It's not an exhaustive list by any stretch of the imagination. One of the things that exacerbated my experience was my lack of self-care which showed up in my life in having a very poor diet and very little exercise. Poor nutrition and lack of movement can have detrimental effects on physiological and mental health and in turn, can make things harder to navigate. If you are experiencing anything that feels like or seems like it could be some form of depression, don't keep it to yourself. I know it's not easy when you're dealing with so much. I have put some resources at the back of this book that you may find helpful.

Are you feeling discouraged? We all go through times of discouragement. There are definitely things that you can do that will lift your thoughts. Thoughts are great perpetrators of discouragement; the voices that we hear whether they come from our enemy or the negative words people have spoken over us have become our own self-talk. We can counteract that self-talk. Take the time to write down words of encouragement to yourself. I have found this invaluable. You can use some of your favourite scriptures and statements of love that speak life over yourself. Rehearse them out loud, pray them. I know this is challenging. This can feel like you're faking it, but don't give up. Put on music that makes you happy. I have a happy song playlist. Whenever I feel that discouragement in my mind and tension in my body, I put it on and I dance and I sing deliberately, or I get outside and just walk and breathe. It is often the complete opposite of what I feel like doing at these times, but once I get started, the release is powerful. It can help clear your mind, energise you and relieve tension. You are worth all the love and care of the Creator of the universe, who has called you the Precious Apple of His eye.

Reflection

Take some time to do this self-check.

- When I wake up in the morning, what is the first thing I think/feel (Don't write down the first religious/spiritual answer that comes to mind. This is a space for complete honesty with yourself.)?

- Are there any thoughts that regularly intrude on my day and how do these make me feel?

- How am I feeling physically right now?

- What am I looking forward to?

- What gives me joy?

- How are my energy levels?

The Breath

Asking for help means I am growing in self-awareness. It means I am learning to love myself and it means I'm stewarding my life and my mental health. It means that I believe that God created humanity to do this journey of life together with Him.

Chapter 7

Touch and Who Touches

What event or person in your life told you that you were worthless or that your contribution to life was of little significance?

These are not easy questions to answer. The truth is the answers to these questions often have layers to them. It is rarely one event or comment that allows this belief to develop and it can be so hard for us to come to terms with the fact that we have these feelings deep inside. In a world that is full of sound bites about being worthy and valuable, it can be hard when we see or hear them, yet we don't feel that they are the truth of how we are experiencing life.

We experience feelings of guilt and inadequacy when we try to declare the affirmations with conviction but feel like we are being untruthful. As human beings, we need to know that we are valued and worthy of love. How many times have you written an affirmation on a Post-It note, stuck it up with the expressed desire to say it every day until you truly believe those words and they become your reality, only to find yourself feeling like you have failed because that voice inside that contradicts them seems so loud. That voice didn't come out of nowhere. That voice has a root and a source. It could be the voice of a parent, or teacher or something we learnt to repeat ourselves because of the lies we internalised as a result of the things we suffered. Trauma teaches us to view ourselves through a distorted lens. We are taught false beliefs about who we are directly through negative words spoken to us, or indirectly by what the treatment we endured implies about us. If those things are repeated often enough, they can become the internal dialogue within us, like an unwelcome meditation.

It's not an accident that Scripture tells us to pay attention to what our thoughts are doing and train them to think about good things (Philippians 4:8). Our minds are powerful. Our thought processes shape the way we view the world. If a child grows up continually hearing that they are stupid, or not good at something, or being constantly overlooked and neglected, it is easy to understand how they can develop a belief system of being incapable and unlovable. The more these thoughts become embedded in their mind, the more they become the truth to that child and the foundation of how they view themselves. Have you ever been stuck in a cycle of comparing yourself to other people, comparing your skills and comparing your looks? This is a self-defeating process, because the more we compare ourselves to others, the more we invariably find fault with ourselves. We can hold ourselves in such low regard that we always get confirmation of our worst beliefs about ourselves. Maybe you were compared to siblings or other students. Of course, this will happen to all of us during our lifetime – it's what humans do. We make comparisons. Somehow we have to change that from being the default setting in our own lives. In this age of social media, we are bombarded with things to compare ourselves to: we compare skills, lifestyles, looks, homes, everything. How do you escape from this constant temptation to see yourself as less, with all that surrounds you, especially if you already struggle with a negative opinion of yourself? One way is to change what you meditate on. It's more than the affirmation on the fridge: it's how you view every aspect of who you are. I know that this does not happen overnight, but you're worth a journey.

As I stated in my introduction, I wrote this song while I was reflecting on my life and when I came to the line, "I feel I'm nothing now, won't someone hold me?", it was interesting to me that it went from feeling that I was nothing to wanting to be held. From the onset of life, human connection and touch are imperative to our well-being. When babies have skin-to-skin contact very early after birth, it has been shown to help their heart rate, decrease anxiety and regulate their temperature. It also has been shown to release oxytocin in mothers and improve their ability to relax. Conversely, touch deprivation in babies and infants can significantly affect development.[3]

Physical touch is something that human beings really benefit from. We were created for human touch and connection. I know this is a tender area for many women; it definitely has been for me. You may have had parents who, for whatever reason, were not affectionate, which resulted in a lack of hugs, or maybe affection was just not shown in that way in your family unit. Or maybe, like me, your early experience of intimate touch was as an object for someone else's sexual pleasure. It was a forbidden, shameful touch that spoke to you of your innate value and that value became that of an object. That real and human need for connection, for touch, became distorted into an ugly thing that told us we were not valuable and our personhood didn't matter, just our body parts. When we have been touched in this way as children, we experience guilt and shame that can lead to self-loathing, blame and condemnation. The seeds sown from the experience of forbidden touch grow deep roots that travel with us throughout our childhood into adolescence and adulthood, so much so that the real need for human connection in touch becomes conflated with sexual intimacy. We can actually form the subconscious belief that the only way that tenderness and touch can be experienced is sexual. The opposite of this is also a reality for some of us, who struggle with being touched at all. We bulk at hugging and avoid touch as much as possible because it elicits such revulsion, anxiety and pain. Talking to someone about this kind of violation is really hard. It's a place of deep embarrassment and shame. As women, we have to really be mindful of where we share these experiences; especially, when we are still deeply wounded and very vulnerable. Not every listening ear is the right ear. You have nothing to be ashamed of because you did nothing wrong. The experience of shame is a lie and it is a lie that you must be freed from. Why? Because that shame and guilt do not belong to you. It belongs to the person who violated your innocence and trust. I won't even try to say that this kind of violation is easy to unravel, because it's not. It's very important to have patience and compassion for yourself. It took me years to shed shame and value my own body to recognise the vampires in our midst that feed off of this particular type of vulnerability. Guard your hearts while you do the work and while you allow love to remove the layers of insecurity and doubt. Cherish that little girl who needed to be loved and held safely. You hold her now. Sometimes we don't think about how much we need physical touch but it is really important and beneficial for us. It doesn't have to be in the romantic sense, just that connection from a living being. It could be your children, friends or family. That connection is something that we thrive on. Having pets has so many psychological benefits, even going for a massage. It seems so minor, but taking care of ourselves is never unimportant.

I have to say, I had a kind of baptism of fire as I became free of this bondage that my childhood abuse had me in. There was a lot of praying and a lot of crying. God did a lot of work in me, but it happened over many years, so don't feel like you have to be in a rush. Everybody's journey is different. Every layer for each of us comes up differently. Not everybody has the same response to things; not everybody develops the same symptoms. Be kind to yourself. Back to the baptism of fire: I had been going through my healing journey for some time and I remember the first time I knew that the final stronghold was about to fall off. I was going to shatter the shame barrier and, let me tell you, the way I was going to do it was through a testimony at church. I had been doing the work and by this point, I had shared my story in small group settings. Now that shame thing had to go. I knew that this was what I had to do. I was no longer willing to own something that didn't belong to me. Anyway, I went up and I gave my testimony. There were tears, but as I spoke I could feel the freedom bursting out of my chest. I felt it and it was like I was saying, "I win. You don't get to triumph over me. I have been given victory. I win." So as you can imagine, it was great and it was a powerful time and I really believe that God used it to break down some barriers to enable others to feel like they were not alone. After the service, a group of us went out to eat and I couldn't believe it when a pastor said to me, "If I were you, I wouldn't have shared a testimony like that in the church, because people would take it and mark you." Those were his exact words. I confess to you that the words that came out of my mouth at that moment were not that sanctified. At that moment, I knew that I was free, because his words ricocheted right off me. I didn't feel shame and I didn't feel embarrassed. I just felt disgusted that he could even have that in his mind. But I was free.

Never doubt that you will experience wonderful things unfold as you grow in freedom. Don't only expect it at the end of the journey because I think there are different levels to this thing. However, as you go along, you may experience lots of small victories and lots of big wins.

Reflection

Questions to Ponder:

- What are the first words that come to mind when I think of me?

- How do I feel about touch?

- How much touch do I have in my life?

- When was the last time I had a hug?

The Breath

Put your hand on your heart and breathe. Speak to that little girl within: "I love you. You are valuable, unique and precious. Your desire to be touched and held is not shameful, it is not wrong. You were created in love, for love and to be loved."

Chapter 8

Soothing Me – The Relief That Brings Pain

We are human beings; beautiful and intricate creatures. We often tend to hold onto our comfort zone, even when the beliefs and habits that make us comfortable can cause us pain in the long run. These habits may offer short-term pleasure but can result in long-term suffering. When I refer to "pleasures", I mean the things that distract us and prevent us from addressing the pain we feel inside.

Life is often challenging, but sometimes we can choose what difficulties we face. Our brains naturally seek comfort in the familiar, such as habits we've formed over time. These habits may have served us well in the past, but it's crucial to examine them to see if they continue to be helpful or have become a hindrance. Sometimes, our habits can become a cage that keeps us from making positive life changes. Recognising this and not letting pain define who we are is necessary. This isn't about blame but rather understanding the power of our minds. I've heard an old story several times. I don't know where it's from, but it goes like this:

"A man goes to the circus and sees a massive elephant tied to a pole by a little rope. The elephant is not moving outside of the parameters that the rope allows. The man asks the workers in the circus how it is possible that this huge creature, who could so obviously tear itself away from this tiny constraint, allows itself to be limited by it. The worker responds, 'When the elephant was small, and we tied him by this rope to the pole, the baby elephant could not move further than the rope allowed. No matter how hard he tried, he was not strong enough to break the restraint. As a result, the elephant was conditioned into thinking that the rope was stronger than him no matter how large he grew.'"

The adult elephant was restraining itself, and the old belief pattern remained even when it was no longer valid. Some of the things we used to believe about ourselves may have been helpful or necessary for a time. The danger happens when we fail to recognise when that thought, idea or belief about ourselves becomes obsolete – a threat to our life. Let me introduce you to Suzy: Suzy had spent years of her life in a tight family circle. She would go to work, go home, sit in front of the TV and eat junk food. After chatting with the family, she would go to bed, and the next day, she would rinse and repeat the same routine. This was the bulk of her existence. One day, Suzy noticed that she felt unhealthy and was unhappy. She started to see things that she might like to try. She began to talk about these ideas with some of her family members whom she loved dearly. Unfortunately, their response was not enthusiastic, as they had a way of doing things, which was their routine. Suzy desired to be healthy, but as she looked around her familiar setting, she realised no one else was interested in trying new things. She had no experiences that told her she could try these things alone. Embarking on these new things seemed too hard without her family, as her identity was intertwined with them as a unit. Suzy had got used to identifying what should be normal for her based on her family. The moment Suzy thought of trying something new, she felt fear and it was easier for her to retreat because it brought relief. Even though the unhealthy lifestyle she was experiencing was making her unhappy, the idea of doing something different without her family was so unfamiliar that lying to herself was easier than enduring the discomfort. For Suzy, the "pleasure" was the feeling of safety.

Do you ever feel like a part of you is constantly searching for relief, trying to ease the pain and discomfort in your life? It's common for babies to get comfort in things like blankets or pacifiers, especially when they're young. However, suppose we grow up feeling emotionally unsafe or in a state of scarcity. In that case, this need for comfort can become distorted and difficult to manage. So, it's important to recognise when we need to soothe ourselves and find healthy ways to do so. Perhaps we experienced physical abuse in the home or learning environment, resulting in this deep chasm from which we must find relief. I used to find relief in food. I distinctly remember being on a diet, one of the many times I tried to lose weight and yet, I was buying biscuits and sitting down with a big mug of tea and just going through a whole packet. This was something familiar to me. On one particular day, I heard clearly within my heart, "You're getting something out of that biscuit. When you work out what you need relief from, you can work out how best to ease and get relief from that thing without hurting yourself." Inevitably, after indulging in the "comfort" of the great food escape, the crashing waves of self-loathing followed soon after.

This began the cycle of self-loathing and self-flagellation. It took the form of overeating because "you're never going to lose the weight anyway", to feeling so sick I'd diet, loving myself as long as I was doing well, rinse and repeat. I was a top-tier legalist. What pleasure causes you pain? Is it a casual relationship with someone you know doesn't value you? Still, you continue because they are familiar, and you can convince yourself you're enjoying your time with them to avoid feeling alone. Have you ever wanted to do something new and exciting but were afraid? Perhaps you've grown accustomed to your current job, even though you hate it because it's familiar and safe. Or you've developed a habit of reading books to find relief, which is great. Still, sometimes, this can become isolating and prevent you from connecting with others. You might tell yourself that you prefer to be alone, but deep down, you crave human connection and new experiences.

This may sound so unlikely, but I know from experience that diving into the pages of books was one of my go-to mechanisms for escaping reality. I still love to read a lot, but not in a way that blocks out the world. You might live in the church building, your whole life revolves around it. You won't miss any gatherings or meetings; you volunteer for everything. This may not be a bad thing in and of itself. However, if this is stopping you from developing in other areas of your life and if you are doing these things to convince yourself that you are good enough, that you are holy enough, that you are worthy of God's love or to validate your existence, the relief you get from feeling safe could mask resentment and regret that comes crashing in later in life. In my teen years, I had no idea who I would be – outside of being a good-time person, the party person in the group, or the person who overindulges in whatever substance or activity that would numb my senses. I did all of these things, even though deep within, I was just stressed, troubled and sitting among all these people, feeling completely disconnected. Those were some conflicting times for me, yet God would show up right in the middle. For example, I had more than a few experiences of random strangers approaching me at house dances asking me what I was doing there and people walking behind me to make sure I got home safely. It was all just some random stuff that I only got answers for years later. I've given thanks for those things a lot since then. It is important to note that seeking relief in the familiar has another aspect. When you begin to examine your desires to change and take steps towards making adjustments – no matter how small – you will have to confront people's perceptions and expectations of you. This can be one of the hardest things to do because people become comfortable with the person they have come to know and the representation of you that they have created in their minds. As you embark on your journey of restoration, it is essential to acknowledge that not everybody will be supportive of your growth and healing. Some people may feel threatened by your changes – even those who love you.

When I wrote the line in the song, "Searching to find relief, these pleasures hurting me", it was as I said, a reflective look on my journey to date and what I realised was, as I progressed slowly in this journey of healing, self-awareness and restoration. My incremental changes were met with varying responses. As you embark on this journey, not only do you have to come to terms with your self-talk, your wounds, and the default settings that you are choosing to change, but you also have to build boundaries that protect you from the effects of other people's opinions and projections upon you. Some people do feel entitled to give their unsolicited opinions about your changes. Still, there will also be those who are lovely, very encouraging and supportive. Remember that not everyone's opinion matters, and you should focus on your growth and well-being.

What are you doing right now? Are you comfy? I need to speak to you, beautiful woman, about the people in your life.

Some of the people who have shared great times with you, and with whom you have even shared your deepest and most intimate fears, may not continue to be a part of your life in the same way as you journey forward. Yes, some of the challenges we face in life are due to our circumstances, while some are because people have become familiar with our broken and insecure parts. They have seen us in moments of doubt, trauma and weakness. Some of our closest friendships were formed out of shared traumatic experiences and while it can be difficult, we must learn to let go of those things that we cling to so tightly. It's not that these people are necessarily bad or hateful, and we must avoid jumping to conclusions and labelling them as such. Sometimes, people grow and change, and we must develop and move forward. If we have bonded with someone based on shared traumatic experiences, it's only natural that things will change as we grow. As you begin to experience genuine love, both for yourself and from others, and grow in acceptance of who you are, you will find yourself walking in a newfound freedom. It's important to remember that this freedom already exists within you. The journey of transforming your mind and heart does not begin from a place of brokenness, but rather from a position of acceptance of all that you have been given. Love, joy and freedom are readily accessible, though it can be challenging to comprehend fully.

Suppose you start from a place of understanding that you are already loved and free. In that case, your journey becomes one of uncovering and unveiling yourself rather than grasping and fighting to climb towards freedom. Each of us will have a unique journey with different tools and methods of achieving growth. Still, the starting point is the same:

acceptance of the love and freedom already within us. This counterintuitive starting point leads to a life of restoration and renewal, where we can truly be free. I must reiterate this point: It can be challenging to accept that relationships can change or end, but it can be freeing when we do so without malice or ill intent towards others. Some relationships will remain strong, while others will fade away naturally. Understanding and accepting this reality is important, even if it is difficult. As we transform our thoughts and become our true selves, it can be hard to accept when someone we rely on for comfort or support begins to withdraw. This is when people can give up for a while and take refuge in the familiar. Change is difficult.

Our true selves are found in Christ and revealed through Him. However, it is not enough to say the words or be religious about it. We must truly accept His love on a deep, intimate level. We often get stuck in a performative mode, trying to be perfect or presenting ourselves in a way we believe others want to see. We beat ourselves up for not being good enough and struggle with our true feelings. This can lead to a cycle of self-punishment and false beliefs. It is necessary to let go of our false selves and embrace who we truly are, even if it means letting go of previously good relationships that now hinder us.

We are created to grow in union with the Divine and to become more interconnected with God and with each other. This growth can only happen through relationships. Therefore, with love, we must let go of some of our most intimate relationships to meet new people, learn from them, and grow. It's important to understand that these shifts do not have to be accompanied by bad feelings or malice and it's OK when someone moves on or when we feel the need to move on. I'm not referring to the superficial pretence we put on where we say all the right things but still feel torn apart inside. I'm talking about the place of true freedom, where we can release all our emotions with joy and without any bitterness or resentment. If you've ever felt hurt or angry about being separated from someone or something, whenever the time comes that you feel ready, take the time to sit in silence and allow the truth of your feelings to surface. Sometimes, we ask for the wrong things in our prayers and only by doing the real work can we confront our flaws and imperfections. We must admit them, be free from guilt and shame and give them to God. We may not know the truth about our own ugliness, but we'll have to face it sooner or later. We can do this through counselling sessions, trusted communities and face-to-face contact with God. There's nothing wrong with wanting to be comforted when we're feeling lost or abandoned. It's time to be there for ourselves and for that part of us that craves love and affection. We're never truly alone, even when we feel unseen or unnoticed.

It's easy to feel like we need to be constantly busy and productive and that we should always be doing something for someone else. But this can lead to insecurity and an unhealthy need to be needed. Big organisations often exploit this need in people, causing them to sacrifice their well-being in a way that is not healthy. It's important to remember that taking care of ourselves is not selfish. We must give ourselves love and care and treat our bodies as precious and valuable. This will have a positive impact on us and those around us. I love that the Holy Spirit is often referred to as the Comforter. It is natural for us to desire comfort and safety, and this is because we are created in the image of God and are meant to share our lives with others. It is not an abstract or unattainable concept to be soothed and comforted by the Spirit. The more we accept our union with God and His absolute delight in us, the easier it becomes to rest in and experience comfort and love.

Reflection

Comfort that hurts us.

Questions to Ponder:

- Where do I seek relief?

- Is my relief habitual?

- Is it hurting me?

The Breath

I am worthy of care. I have the choice and the power to change the habits that no longer work for my good.

Chapter 9
Learning, Unlearning, Re-learning

Right from our birth, we enter the world ready to be moulded into who we are. We rely on our mothers and fathers to tell us who we are; our environments, our diet, and the culture we are born into, to tell us our stories. In some ways, the whole pursuit of life is discovering the answer to this question. We were reliant on external sources, so whatever those external experiences brought to us, shaped our very minds. Our experiences have shaped us; the things said to us, the things we have suffered and the things we were told (even without words by society). We can learn a lot by observing the people who get praised and those we treat with disdain in our society. We have learnt our value and worth by the value and worth given to us by the people and places we encountered. The very way your brain works and the neurological pathways that are formed begin to shape who you are and by that, we become the total of our habits: habits we build, the way we speak, the actions we take, the people we hang around with. All of our habits become a person and sadly, they are the things that tell a story in the world. I can say we have been lied to. The story that has unfolded in our pain and our trauma has closed our eyes to the true value that we have. So we continue to look for people to teach us and unfortunately, we sometimes look in the wrong places. I remember being in secondary school, pursuing music from primary age, playing instruments and loving classical music – just instrumentation, i.e. living in the music department. I enjoyed that place, messed about with various instruments and loved being in that world of music-making. Unfortunately, when I was going to school, that was not "cool." I got to the age of about fourteen and started to have a crisis of identity.

Now remember, I'm saying this in hindsight: I had no idea I was having a crisis of identity. I had no idea that my woundedness as a child played so much a part in the insecurity of my need to be liked and my need to be understood and accepted. So I decided to take a journey into what I thought the culture of the school and the people around me wanted a fourteen-year-old black girl to look like, which resulted in me branching into new friendship groups. I juggled two friendship groups and had two lives. I was the person that did the things I enjoyed and this other persona was a bit more rebellious, exuberant, and bunking off, i.e., "truanting." I was exploring and getting into trouble. I didn't get into any terrible trouble because deep down, I knew this was not me, so I made sure I did my homework (for the most part) and my schoolwork and kept up doing the things I knew I wanted to. I know this is not unique to me; it is something most teenagers go through as they try to find identity, and part of the whole journey as an adolescent is to try out different things to see what fits. I searched for others to show me who I was; this is what we do. We search for those external relationships to inform our identity. Our true identity cannot be found in external things. Yet we use the external as an identifier, which is why, when things happen to us that cause damage and are devastating to us, they can become our identity. We experience shame and internalise it by believing we are shameful; we carry guilt that is not ours. We become the product of somebody else's ill-treatment. Some places we look to to learn about who we are, are deficient. We need to learn, read books and explore; that's how we grow. We learn things that seem reasonable for a while and then may discover they are not beneficial, so we seek a better way. We must be determined to stay open to learn new things. I can't tell you how much the process of life will cause you to do that. We all can think of at least one thing we used to do or believe until we got a deeper understanding of it and changed our minds.

You may have reached a place where you have become comfortable with yourself. But if the way you see yourself is still wrapped up in your pain and your trauma, can you genuinely believe that you have seen who you could fully be? I say that because a new version of us is revealed with every new depth of learning about ourselves and healing. We see the updated version emerge only when we are willing to let go of our former selves and some ideas we had about ourselves. You're going to hit things that shake your former ways of thinking and understanding yourself, where it will feel like you must change and evaluate or die on the hills of, "I have always been this way", "This is how I've always done it" and "This is how I've always thought." We know many people who will gladly stagnate on any or all of those hills. Now, I suppose I should put a little disclaimer that, yes, there are a few unchangeable things that we have always done in the same way; a few unchanging truths (but very few, I think, and we're not talking about these). You can shift and pivot and change the way you do almost anything. The choice is yours. No matter what it feels like, you are under no obligation to remain the same, no matter what friends, colleagues, or family say. You can learn a thing, then unlearn it and relearn something else because you can change your mind. Your willingness to do this will help you change your perspective on yourself. I see the line of this song, "Won't someone teach me", as the cry of our hearts: the child rejected or misused or overlooked, expressing their discontent in tantrums and perceived disobedience, the teenager trying to find her way, trying to understand her place in the world, looking in the mirror and not liking what she sees and feeling the peer pressure to conform to an image that is not comfortable to her. It's the woman feeling like an outcast because she doesn't look like the preferred image that she sees on social media; the woman who has masked her whole life, burying her wounds, doubts and fears to find them assailing her days and crashing into her life in her older years, having performed various roles to find identity and value, yet seeing the minimal reward for all her efforts. All of these still scream from the void, "Someone please show me that I am precious. Show me that my life is worth something. Show me that I am beautiful. Show me that I am valuable. Show me that I have a purpose. Show me that I am not just surplus to requirements. Show me that I am worthy."

The thing is, no matter how much our external world seems to validate us – no matter the accolades, no matter the friends, no matter the financial enrichment, no matter what external experience – if we deep down have not come to the truth of our innate value, nothing can satisfy us. The only thing that will bring us to a place of freedom is a change of our minds, a transformation, a reforming, a renewal.

Teachers are incredible; I am grateful for those who have entered my life and helped me learn. They taught me how to listen, study, inquire and investigate. If we are open to learning, there are many ways we are taught, so being able to ask for help is a powerful thing. That heart cry must, at some stage, be voiced outside of ourselves, which can be terrifying. I know it makes you feel vulnerable and safer to have the turmoil inside where nobody else can see it. You don't want to expose yourself to another person. The thing is, we cannot truly grow in love and learn to love ourselves without vulnerability. Your openness to see a new way, brings a new kind of vulnerability. It's not one of victimhood but one that is born of courage and the willingness to take the risk of exposing your wound, the mess of it and the smell of it so that it can be cleaned, dressed and fully tended to. We have believed the lie that to be valuable and worthy, we must appear unblemished. We should be ashamed of our humanity and feel some embarrassment because of the pain we experienced that was not our own doing. You are not weak if you ask for help. This myth that you must be able to carry the load all on your own without telling anyone and work it out, is hurting you and it is complete nonsense! I am so glad that we are living in times when therapy and counselling are spoken about more freely. Things are changing slowly, but they are changing. Different forms of treatment and organisations can provide support throughout the process, providing access to beneficial tools. Therapy/counselling is not a dirty word. It is not a sign of a lack of faith. And it is not, as some describe it, "navel-gazing." It can be a confidential listening ear and a place that gives you space to work through your challenges and supports you as you form healthier ways of thinking and being. You can find resources in various forms: books, podcasts, etc. There are so many ways to access information. Feel free to process in collaboration. Talking to someone is invaluable. If you don't have a safe place or someone you trust, find an excellent counselling service. Organisations that have a good sense of community can also be helpful. First and foremost, you must feel safe. If you are not ready yet, these pages are just there for you to use to express whatever you need so that you can revisit them.

My healing journey began when I understood that God already loved me. The steady, consistent nudge of God was the beginning of my conscious choice to learn how to take better care of myself. My support came in so many ways in the form of trusted friends and a lot of time on my own in prayer, weeping, wailing and reading. The Holy Spirit took me step-by-step through my process. Sadly, I was often advised not to read anything like psychology because it would be dangerous. I'm so glad I was more curious than afraid. The "still small voice" inside that told me it was OK, won the battle. I know that the elders who gave me that advice, had my best interests at heart. However, I am grateful for the various people from different walks of life and other denominational perspectives who were there at different times along the way. The beautiful thing is that your worth, your value and how much you are loved are not determined by anything that has happened to you. It is not defined by how you think of yourself or your behaviour. The world does not even choose it. One thing that determines your worth is that you are God's child, loved and in union with Him. You have received the grace to go through this renewing and transforming journey of truly seeing yourself as you are seen. Not as you will be seen when you sort your life out, but how you are seen right now with all that you carry and with all your experiences. You are entirely accepted, loved and precious. The goal is for that truth to come alive within you.

Reflection

Questions to Ponder:

- Who do I feel safe to ask for help?

- Can they support me?

- Am I determined to deal with my pain all alone? Why?

The Breath

I am grateful that my worth and value are unquestioned. Right now, exactly as I am, I am fully loved, accepted and beautiful.

Chapter 10

Back Here Again – the Stalls, the Stops, the Restarts

So you started the work. You started looking into yourself and walking towards loving yourself, changing thoughts and habits and you're doing well. You're doing amazingly; you're changing. Things are changing. You feel like you're beginning to understand yourself and know the parts of your personality and your thinking process that need retraining. But suddenly, you find an old habit or way of thinking that starts to invade your day: You wake up one morning and find you feel low, your mind is clouded and you have no motivation. Or you begin to feel the old feelings of worthlessness. Something happens, and you seem to fall into the old cycle and that voice that you know so well starts to whisper, "You haven't changed," "All this stuff you're doing is not working. What's the point? You can't change. This behaviour is who you really are." You can start to add your own monologue, "I knew it. I've tried different things. I started to feel healthy and have fallen off. I have spoken affirmations and none of it's working. I might as well just leave it and not bother with it. It's not working."

Somebody should've told us that this journey is not linear. It is a journey of discovery; sometimes, it can feel like three steps forward and two steps back. The repeating and the retraining can sometimes feel like a slow walk through a vat of treacle. The old way we have been conditioned became habitual and breaking that habitual thought process does not happen overnight. Imagine your whole life has been shaped. Your brain has been shaped and has made pathways to prioritise these negative thoughts and to prioritise the old way of being. So, as you go on this journey, there will be times when you will have setbacks. How we were shaped, how we lived our lives and what we thought were automatic took years to learn. They will take unravelling. You will have to learn to accept that you have been given grace, the ability, strength and peace through the love of God, and give that grace to yourself. I imagine you're asking what it means to give grace to yourself. It means to accept yourself in your entirety, and the way you can do that is to know that you are accepted in your entirety. Does this mean that no undesirable parts of your behaviour or nurturing need transformation? Of course not, but it means that the grace of God encompasses your whole being, the good and the not-so-good parts because you are known fully. You are known and loved, giving you the space to release all parts of yourself into the hands of Love. So I would say to give yourself grace means to be honest about who you are in your entire being. That can be uncomfortable as you start to see less desirable parts of yourself and as you start to become aware of your selfishness or your pride or your self-pity. It can be hard to come face-to-face with yourself. Still, it's the only way to start loving that little girl; that teenager who was confused and seemingly out of control. It's the only way to love the woman you are right now with all her faults, fears and desires. Good and bad, love her into life and into becoming the woman you want her to be. That does not mean excusing or making excuses for bad choices. I have often had conversations with myself and other women where I recognise our excuses for bad behaviour; excuses we make for how we made other people feel, or unacceptable things. We are not excusing these things; we can know the reasons without making excuses. That place of acceptance is profound and needful. It goes hand in hand with accountability: It says you accept that the things you were going through caused you to behave in ways that have sometimes hurt other people. You can acknowledge that and, where possible, make amends for those things without engaging in self-flagellation. I'm committed to allowing myself to be loved and to live. I'm committed to doing the work of self-observation. It's hard to work on it and self-observation hurts. You could be tempted to feel shame or embarrassment at some of your past behaviours, thoughts, or feelings, but it's only in that discomfort that we can find freedom. So you feel like you're back at the place you thought you had left behind, but you're not; if this is where you are right now, you're not back in the same place you were in the past. The well-embedded habits try resetting themselves, but you have moved forward. You now have new tools, and the fact that you recognise a pattern arising, proves that you are no longer in the same place you were.

One of the things I've learnt on this journey is that we should pay attention to our feelings. We should acknowledge our feelings, but we should also question our feelings, where they come from, and whether they are telling us the truth. I am saying that if the thoughts you are experiencing at these times identify you based on an old program, they're not what God says about you; they are not the truth. You are beloved and wonderfully made; you are beautiful and precious. You can do challenging things. You know you can, because you've done it before and will do it again. In these times, we must rest in our faith the most and trust that all things are at work in us for our ultimate good. What we believe is often wholly opposed to how we feel and what the programme of our mind tells us. The mind is made new when it has new food and – in the brain's case – new thoughts to conform to. I'm quite aware that I often use food as an example. It's just because of my journey with food that it has become an indicator of where I am in my mind. When I am present and content, I take care of my body. I recognise the things my body doesn't like and that are not healthy and I exercise. Part of my taking care of myself is being aware of what I eat. So, If I notice my eating pattern starts to shift to the opposite of what is good for me, I recognise something is off, and I have to pay attention. Am I tired or stressed? Did I eat something my body doesn't agree with, or do my thoughts need to be adjusted? I recognise that sugar has been a place of comfort for me, so I actively and intentionally change my mind. Everyone has their weak areas. The point is to be in tune and self-aware so you can make adjustments rather than berate yourself. Beginning to take care of yourself when you have learnt to ignore your needs may seem selfish or self-absorbed at first. Taking time to examine what's happening inside, through therapy, or time away from church activities, social media, or work, just for yourself may feel strange. I've got a pair of Adidas trainers, and the laces say self-care is not selfish; I bought them because of those laces!

When I'm speaking about self-care, I'm not talking about going to a spa or getting your hair and nails done (although doing these things is an excellent part of self-grooming). But even those things can be something we do to show people externally that we are on top of our game. I am talking about the self-care that says "no" when you feel like somebody may look at you unfavourably; self-care that causes you to notice that you need more sleep, so turn down an invitation. You must show up for yourself because showing up for yourself will also benefit those around you. You won't do this perfectly, but the aim is not perfection – it's wholeness. It is a process of repeating and repeating until the new thinking becomes muscle memory. A lot of us like instant things, we like instant change, we want instant gratification. One of the hardest things we can learn as humans is to delay gratification and accept that only some results will be experientially instant. You have exchanged an old life for a new one and are growing into a new reality. Be patient with yourself.

I watched a recent documentary about an incredible athlete with a vast natural talent that nobody could deny. As I watched the rigorous training and the many injuries he sustained – one of which forced him to take several weeks off of training – his coach said even though he had worked hard for months with intense training, having those couple of months off for recovery set him back so much, that it would be like starting from scratch. However, because of the training that he had been through before his injury, his muscles had memory. Although it was tough starting the process again, those muscles knew what to do. He wasn't starting from scratch in the same way as somebody who had never trained in that way before. You are not starting from scratch when you have a perceived setback. You're starting from a place of new knowledge. You're just repeating, and that is part of learning, relearning, discarding things that don't work and picking up new stuff. You are growing.

Reflection

There is power in repetition.

Having to repeat an action until it becomes a habit is not failure: it's part of the process.

Questions to Ponder:

- What are the undesirable habits that I find myself falling back into?

- What do I tell myself when I notice this happening?

- How can I accept myself and show up for myself when this happens?

The Breath

I receive God's grace and love, knowing that I am fully accepted and fully loved right where I am. I receive grace daily to accept myself as I am, while learning to flourish in the truth of my identity as a loved, healed and restored woman.

Chapter 11

Being Seen and the People That Are Sent to Us

My healing journey started with my eyes being open to God's love. This fact ignited a sense in me that I was valued outside of anything I had done, anything that any person did to me and anything I ever said. I didn't stop to do any work immediately after coming to faith. I was beginning to realise some of the experiences that I couldn't explain when I was younger, could now be explained by the fact that God was present with me. Even before I understood anything about the presence of God, looking back, I saw so many things that pointed me to His presence.

I was His. I was not an accident of birth. I was not an afterthought. The Creator called me precious. I was seen. No matter where you are with your faith, you are loved. We stepped into the reality of receiving a gift that means we can relinquish the human need to carry everything ourselves, feeling like we are solely responsible for the outcome; Christ has taken care of the outcome and we are in union with God.

To be seen is one of the biggest things we need as humans – besides food and clothing at the shelter. Children need to be seen; they need to feel that their emotions are important and that they're being accepted and acknowledged by their caregivers.

Interconnectedness in relationships is how we approach this. I'm so grateful for the people I believe have been sent to me.

Some of the people who have come into our lives have been damaging. When I speak about the people sent to us, I don't always talk about the things that seemed pleasant about those people. Now, don't get me wrong, I'm not talking about abusive people. I don't adhere to the belief that God has sent some people to bring destruction into our lives to teach us a lesson so that we can grow stronger. What I do believe is that there is evil in the world. And through His relationship with us, God works in us to bring about good. The hard things, the cruel things that we go through and experience can all be completely transformed.

We never know the people who will bring good things into our lives. They don't always stay for long and often, only after they have moved on, for whatever reason, do we recognise the importance and value of those people who have been sent to us. It could be as simple as someone who encouraged you right when you needed it or helped you financially when you didn't ask and thought nobody knew your need.

Some interactions with people feel uncomfortable at the time. Sometimes, they say things to you that you find painful and quite hard, but upon reflection, you realise that those words were necessary and helped you move to a different place.

There were times when I felt isolated and couldn't deal with being around people. This manifested in my life as going out to events but then retreating to spend most of my time alone. I needed this alone time to deal with my internal struggles and pains. However, I also made mistakes and didn't have the proper boundaries, which caused me to spend myself in my attempts to please God. I was subconsciously trying to earn what was already mine, and this delayed my internal journey to come to grips with who I am.

Sometimes we can use busyness as an excuse to avoid confronting ourselves. We feel good about what we've done and enjoy bringing value to others' lives, but this alone will not let us feel truly seen. We may be physically seen by people, but they may not see us for who we truly are. However, along the way, we encounter people who are meant to remind us that we are not alone. They may not be everyone we meet, but they are there to help us on our journey.

God sees you and I hope you feel seen in these pages.

It is a challenging, vulnerable and uncomfortable place to let people see you; to know that you are opening yourself up to potential judgement and being misunderstood. It's accepting the possibility that people may reject this new you. Love is vulnerability.

"To be seen and acknowledged is a fundamental need and desire of every person. We are created to live, move and work together in a community. We are created to give and receive from each other and connect deeper. This desire and need does not diminish as we age. As we grow older, we tend to have fewer people in our inner circle, but we still need those individuals with whom we can be our authentic selves. Authenticity is a buzzword these days, but we can only achieve true authenticity once we are honest with ourselves. Part of being seen is seeing ourselves and coming to terms with the fact that we may not be as kind or good as we think. It can be a tough realisation, but it's not meant to condemn us. Rather, it's about acknowledging the areas where we need to grow and change."

No matter how virtuous we may seem when we intentionally explore the truth within us, we will inevitably confront ourselves and be challenged by what we discover. In the new season of our lives, some of us are waiting for the real us. We will go through different phases and transitions and must accept and embrace these changes. If we desire to experience freedom and healing, we must move through these phases and allow ourselves to change.

As we look back on different phases of our lives, we may notice that the people around us also change. Some people who were once close to us may become distant, which can be difficult to accept. However, if we choose to do the inner work of healing and accept our freedom, we will encounter change. We must let go of the need for things to stay the same and embrace the fact that people and circumstances will change. We must relinquish our old identity in exchange for our true identity.

I remember vividly a day I was in prayer when the question came to mind: "If you could not sing any more, who would you be?" I tell you now, when the question arose inside, I had to pause and think. If all I am is hinged on what my gift is or what I am doing for work, if that thing changes or is removed or something happens that prevents me from doing it any more, my life would crumble. That was one of those standout moments in my life that I can pinpoint because it highlighted to me that my identity and my value must be something more. It must be something deeper and must be rooted in something bigger than myself. Who we truly are is much more than what we do. Your true identity is not defined by the titles you hold, the roles you play, or your job identifiers. Although people often describe us by what we do, our worth and value remain intact even if these things are taken away from us. Therefore, our identity and worth must be based on something else. As a woman, your value comes from being a child of God. These days, our value is often determined by external factors such as likes, followers and streams, but in the past, value was measured differently (such as having a family, a home or graduating from school). While these things may mark certain phases in our lives, they do not determine our worth.

Although I have an intimate sense of closeness with God, there have been times when I didn't feel that at all. During some of my darkest days, I would let loose in my prayers, asking earnestly, "Where are you? Do you actually see me?" I have had many doubts and questions and even when I fluctuated in my confidence in my identity as someone loved by God, I would always, not of my own volition, be brought back to a sense of belonging. Despite my outbursts, doubts, fears and offence at the suggestion that I was seen by the Creator of the universe and yet suffering, I was always reminded of my worth by this sense of belonging.

If there are times when you feel unseen, even by God, I hear you. You don't need to be afraid during these moments, because God doesn't relate to you based on the person you pretend to be but rather loves who you truly are, imperfections and all. When you pray, it's OK to be honest and authentic; there's no need for fancy religious prayers. In that space of vulnerability, you can freely express what's happening inside. You may not even have words, but that's OK; you can sit in silence with the assurance of God's love. In your silence, He hears you.

When I was young, I had two children before the age of twenty-five. I remember being at my first church, where there were quite a few 'older women – the "mothers of the church." Some of them could see me and others were quite damaging to me. We must distinguish honouring people from expecting that, because they are older, they have nothing to learn or any healing of their own to do. A couple took the time to speak to me; they said things that seemed way beyond my capacity, which I respectfully dismissed in my mind at the time. I was highly sensitive and susceptible to being offended and wounded by words, especially as they hit an already damaged and bruised place.

Some of the things said were hard, and the delivery left a lot to be desired. In retrospect, a lot of the things that some of these women said to me were valuable and I know their intentions were good. I had to let go of the wrapping of the delivery so that I could get to the meat of what they were saying. I was only able to do that after a period of healing. Letting go is essential.

When I was about fourteen, my English teacher was amazing. She was terrifying and warm at the same time. I wanted to hear everything she had to say, but everybody else thought she was a dragon, so I felt like I had to behave like I thought she was a dragon, too. She made me feel like she could see into the depths of my soul when she looked at me, so I was afraid to look into her eyes, even though I loved her class. I loved listening to her voice. She would point out how I adapted myself to suit certain groups, ask me pointed questions about books I was reading and things I enjoyed and commented on my choices. I hid from her a lot when I would've liked to spend more time talking to her; I wish I had. We all need someone like that in our lives. I don't know that I appreciated it then, but I know some of the things she said formed some of the building blocks in my life that I later recognised. She didn't know the lies I carried; maybe she did. Whatever the case, she was there at that stage of my life to speak to the young woman I was created to be. She spoke truth into my inward parts even in my ignorance.

These were only a few of the people who were sent to me. At the time I was absolutely oblivious, but I'm so grateful for them now.

Reflection

Take a moment to reflect on the people in your life and your relationships with them.

Questions to Ponder:

- Can you identify the individuals who support you and actively listen to you?

- Can you also identify those who bring you down and detract from your sense of self-worth?

The Breath

2 Timothy 2:13

"If we are faithless, He remains faithful, for He cannot disown Himself..."

Take a deep breath.

Chapter 12
Gentle Perseverance

"Now I'm restored, my strength, my mind renewed."

The line in this song is both true and yet to become true. This line in the song is both true and yet to become true. It perfectly demonstrates what I was writing about and reflecting upon. The truth in my experience is that I am becoming increasingly free, step-by-step, and changing my position concerning myself. At the same time, I understand that there is still a fullness of restoration that I have yet to experience. It is a declaration of faith. This is the position we will maintain throughout our journey. We must hold these two things in tension, which can be quite challenging. You need to know that as you restore your strength and renew your mind, you can take this walk with God in prayer.

You must grow in the understanding of how much you are loved and remember that the Holy Spirit, who is called the Wonderful Counsellor, will guide you as you embark on the journey of self-work or seeking support from a therapist. Whichever path you choose to uncover your wounds and heal them, the truth is, that it is a journey of momentum and gentle perseverance. You will face challenges and changing habits takes time; you have been given the gift of wholeness. Each stage of peeling back the layers of your wounds uncovers another place for restoration and building strength. When I wrote this song in 2010, I had already come a long way from where I started. I had never experienced that level of freedom and understanding of myself before. However, in 2024, as I write these words, I am a completely different person from who I was in 2010. I have reached another level of freedom and understanding of myself that I never thought was possible. I believe this was a gift from God – the One who loves me dearly. But I had to go through the process of shedding my old ways of thinking and being.

It was not an easy road, with bumps, peaks and troughs, but I maintained momentum and held onto the hope of something better. I want you to experience something better and, once you do, you won't settle for the bitterness you once had. Even if it's just in a small area of your life, once you've tasted a different reality, your heart won't be content with returning to what you once knew. This is the momentum you need to keep going: not perfection or a seamless movement, but a taste that gets into your mindset, reminding you that there is more. No matter the obstacles, challenges, or setbacks, the freedom you've glimpsed – waking up in the morning, feeling the sun on your face and feeling hopeful – will help you to keep going. You'll begin to uncover the woman you were truly created to be, bit by bit, shedding the shroud of wounds, bruises, scars and pressures. I believe in gentle perseverance. While some aspects of our lives can be changed instantly, most of us are on a journey of discovery. It's about growing, adapting, seeing, exploring, learning and re-learning.

As human beings, we are supernatural creatures created in love and meant to live in love. I believe that we can know our Creator through faith and that this journey is about discovering the fullness of God in Jesus. Grace has been freely given to the whole cosmos and we are already so deeply loved. "God so loved the world" that He made a way for us to know ourselves in relation to Him and the love and grace freely given is the pathway to unlock complete renewal and transformation. People can help us along the way, but I believe that all is in Christ. This life is beautiful and it's for us to ask questions, to look, and to gently persevere without judging ourselves for our tender areas. We should not judge ourselves for the time it takes or think we should've been further by now. These things are not being inflicted on us by God. The critical voice in our head, the inner critic, or whatever name you want to give to that part of yourself that has an old language or law, is not from God. As we take small steps forward, we may feel like we're going backwards and that's when that voice berates us and tells us that we should be better by now. We must gently persevere and not let that voice hold us back.

I find spiritual language used in the Bible really helpful. For example, when it talks about the "Kingdom", it refers to its presence within and around us. The Kingdom is here and yet to come, and the same goes for restoration and healing. We are being healed, restored and renewed despite the ongoing process. We are both a finished work of art and a work in progress. This can seem confusing, but it's not. Even in a bad place, we can look back and see growth and change. As we become more aware of ourselves and the things that affect us, we can shift and grow; even if it's small or incremental.

We have been invited into a relationship with the fullness of God and adopted into a life with the Creator. In this life, we are whole and healed, with nothing lacking. It is a walk-in union with God: we accept our true identity and shed the layers of experience and damage accumulated from living in the world, allowing more light to illuminate the dark corners of our lives. We come to the truth to make sense of our emotions and behaviours. As we do so, we grow into who we are; into the reality of what it means to be truly human. It can be hard to accept that change. Transformation comes through habitual thoughts and practices. While it may sound clinical or dull, the truth is that we're made up of the things we think, feel and experience. Our thoughts can lead to our emotions and the things we allow ourselves to see can shape our perspective. Romans 12:2 says it like this,

> *"Do not conform to the pattern of this world, but be transformed by the renewing of your mind; then you will be able to test and approve what God's will is..."*

Growing into newness is about building upon the things we practice every day, the things we say to ourselves and the thoughts we think. It's important to observe ourselves, to look at ourselves objectively and to see our thoughts and emotions as an outsider looking in. This allows us to see our habits and thoughts more clearly, and to replace negative thoughts with positive ones. Often pain, abuse or abandonment obscure our perspective. Our lens is dirty and clouded, preventing us from seeing things clearly. However, understanding who we are in Christ can give us a clean lens. It allows us to see ourselves more clearly and experience positive change and transformation. As I started to understand myself better, I became even more grateful that the Gospel is not about earning enough merit to be accepted by God. Sometimes, the way it is preached may give the impression otherwise, but that couldn't be farther from the truth.

"The Spirit of God gently whispers, 'You are free. I have healed your bones, borne your wounds and carried away your pain. Now, you are free to walk through the process of acknowledging, seeing and releasing those things. You can let them go and move forward with your life.'"

There is a power in not identifying with the old you, but it doesn't mean that you don't love her. Your old self deserves to be loved because she carried you through all your challenges, fears and doubts. She got you this far with her resilience and perseverance. Now is the time to love her and let her go, so you can embrace the beautiful woman you are right now. As you continue your journey of growth, development and freedom, remember to cherish your old self and the strength she gave you.

Be gentle with yourself in your perseverance. Don't listen to the voices that tell you that you should be further along, because that doesn't help you to accept where you are. Acceptance of where you are is what propels you to keep going.

As we look around and observe and see the facts, we're not in the business of denying facts or reality. We just have a different reality, running alongside the reality that everybody else sees, and so it is the embracing of the true reality that leads to freedom. Our thoughts form the foundation of our being ("As a man thinks, so is he." Proverbs 23:7). Everything in our whole body sends signals to our mind, and it's so powerful that it affects our whole system. When we are feeling a certain way, when we are experiencing things from the outside, it's how we process them in the mind that affects us. It's how they trigger thoughts that turn into feelings. We're talking about the transformation of our lives. A golden aim is to build a momentum of thoughts, actions and beliefs that align with the woman you're becoming, that align with who you truly are. And it can be like dreaming, because when you see the changes in yourself, when you notice that this thing no longer weighs on you the way it did, when you're experiencing more peace and more joy, it's like a waking dream. And it's possible for you. It is possible for you to wake up and experience a day in a completely different way than you have done before, because you have come to understand how your thoughts, the way you eat and the way you move on the earth inform your being. Breaking away from the things that informed your captivity is the thing that enables you to walk in freedom.

Reflection

Think about the ways in which you have kept persevering.

Questions to Ponder:

- What are they things that helped you?

- What have you found unhelpful?

The Breath

I can rest in the middle of my changes. I am not alone.

Chapter 13

God Delights in Our Wholeness

I am deeply grateful. As we come to the end of this song, it feels like the culmination of a period in my life. We often hear about the benefits of gratitude and being thankful. Still, it can be difficult to practice when we are going through tough times. However, no matter what stage of life we are in, we can take a moment to think about something we are thankful for, no matter how small. It's essential to speak these things out loud and to meditate on the good stuff, even when they feel few and far in between.

Take a moment now to think of something you are thankful for.

Have you ever noticed how easy it is to wake up in the morning and immediately start worrying about all the difficult things happening in your life? It's overwhelming when you're bombarded with worries, anxieties, cares and stresses right from the moment you open your eyes. That's why I've been working hard to practice gratitude and thankfulness deliberately and intentionally. Although it can be challenging at times, I understand the importance of paying attention to where our mind is focusing, staying positive and appreciating the good things in life. Even if you're feeling exhausted, it's important to remember that you're not alone. Do you feel like you have been struggling for too long and are beyond tired of it? I know that place very well; you want to throw your hands up and go and eat cake (Oh no, wait... that's me!).

Trust me, even if you don't want to hear this, expressing gratitude and thanks can make a big difference. As the saying goes, "Count your blessings, name them one by one." This practice powerfully shifts our focus and mindset. This doesn't mean all our problems disappear, but it positively changes our hearts and minds. When we focus on being thankful, we realise the simple things we often take for granted, such as being able to breathe, move and have friends. Gratitude has the power to transform our lives and create a thankful heart. We can't wait for thankfulness to come to us, but we must actively seek things for which we are grateful. We should deliberately look for things to remember to be thankful for, such as shelter, food, clothing, good health or anything else we are fortunate to have. Our minds tend to focus on negative things, so training our minds to think positively is a must. As mentioned in the scripture, we should think about things that are good, true and lovely (Philippians 4:8). This is because there is real power in what we set our minds on, and being thankful for even the smallest and simplest things can change our perception and how we see the world around us. I've found that entertaining the lies and all the difficulties in my mind and meditating and rehearsing those didn't make me feel better, it didn't help in any way, and became like an automatic go-to place. One thing that you can do, which I find helpful, is to take a moment to breathe and give thanks as you open your eyes in the morning, before you get out of bed. God takes pleasure in your wholeness and takes pleasure in you just the way you are. This has nothing to do with your level of perfection or whether everything in your life is sorted out. He loves you simply because. He is love and you are His. Abba God is always there for you, and He loves you dearly.

Psalm 18:19 says,

"He brought me into a spacious place; He rescued me because He delighted in me."

God's desire for you is to bring you to a place of freedom where you can recognise and live out this freedom as your reality. This is not just a "sense" of freedom but a true one that always leads you back to the love of God. Love is the root of everything, and it is so all-encompassing and powerful that it wants to consume our lives and flood every area, including every dark corner, with light. We hear the word "love" all over the place. Still, it is dangerous and easy to become desensitised to it because many people say "love", but their actions do not represent love. This causes us to misinterpret what love is to our detriment. Some people use love as a coverall excuse for their actions, which strips the power of love. Love is not just a word, it is an action that should be demonstrated.

Love has become something to see in romantic films, so I think a big part of this journey for us is to rediscover love and passion, rediscover the passion of God and what it means to show love to ourselves and others. Essentially, that's it. That's the journey and we will be ebbing and flowing in its lessons our whole lives. I believe this journey is to grow in discovery and reach maturity in perfect Love. It is said that "perfect love drives out fear... the one who fears is not made perfect in love" (1 John 4:18).

It's a profound statement as we experience various situations, and we are aware of all the emotions that arise. There is something powerful about the impact of love on us. It is a beautiful exercise to think of Love as God. We were created in Love and in the image of Love. Love resides within us, and we are in constant communication with Him. How can we say we are worthless? Love and compassion for yourself will enable you to be thankful. When you look at yourself with empathy, you can give thanks for every incremental win, and for the wins you have yet to see; give thanks for that dream in your heart. Beautiful woman, you are walking into Love, and that love is breaking down hurts; Love is pouring through all your tender parts, breaking through your calluses and freeing you, to be honest. When you look in the mirror, and you may wince at what you see, Love is not wincing; Love is not turning His eye from you.

If you're rolling your eyes about giving thanks for the things you haven't seen yet, I want to encourage you that there are many things I hoped for that weren't in my vision at all. They were simple things, like not having to calculate the shopping as I walked around the supermarket or wanting my existence to make a difference. I also hoped for a time when I was free from the cloud that invaded my life, but I had no idea what that would look like. Despite this, I used to get up – on good days – and say thank you for the things I hadn't seen yet, such as my health, strength, a roof over my head and freedom from fear. I used to say these things even when they weren't true in my experience, but I still hoped for them. No matter how small your steps are and despite everything that is happening in your life right now, there is a version of you that you have not yet seen. I'm grateful for that version of you, that woman who will unfold as you shed the layers that have held you back, that have made you fearful and small. Let's give thanks for the future version of yourself, the one who is waiting just ahead.

Reflection

Question to Ponder:

- When you hear the word "gratitude" and think about thankfulness, what immediately comes to mind?

The Breath

Every person comes to any given situation with their own perception and biases. Healing and restoration enable us to become aware of our own lens and make it clearer.

I am thankful that God is Love. I was created in Love, I was made in the image of Love, I am filled with Love, Love is in me and flows through me.

Chapter 14
Your Freedom Can Be Seen –
See Yourself Free

The crescendo of this song represents a declaration of freedom. It's a message to the outside world and to myself that I am no longer confined. This is my way of telling the world and those who have supported me that I acknowledge their contribution to shaping who I am today. I am embracing the new version of myself. You have to embrace each new version of yourself because it will not look like the past version. You can adapt to the new version of yourself. The truth is that it's not a "new version" in the sense that everything about you, like your hair or where you live, may change. However, inwardly, your true self and identity begin to take up more space. You begin to see the truth of the persona you made for your subconscious protection. You begin to see the beauty of who God made you and the truth of who you are in Christ. You begin to stretch out. Freedom, peace and healing always originate from within. The work that needs to be done is always inside-out. However, the problem is that we often create a false external persona to navigate life on our behalf instead of embracing our true selves. Only when we fall in love with the person we truly are can we journey into the depths of our hearts and minds and face our habits, doubts, fears, anxieties and traumas. As we follow this path, we expand and discover the beloved one of God within.

Your freedom and healing radiate from you and are felt by those around you. Your liberation is magnetic and palpable. The little girl you comforted, the teenager you consoled, the people you forgave – they all felt your compassion. When you look at yourself with love, forgiveness, mercy and compassion, you see yourself through the eyes of God. God sees you with forgiveness, mercy, compassion and unconditional love. You don't have to tell anyone about it; they will see and feel it themselves. Some will find it beautiful and refreshing, while others may feel threatened by it as they meet a new version of you that they are not familiar with. I can confidently say that I am no longer bound but free. I have accepted that I am free, and nothing behind me is holding me back. Although my mind sometimes retreats to old habits, and I experience moments of anxiety or nervousness, those things no longer define my identity. Previously, I used to identify myself with my shame, fear, anxiety, lack of self-control and addictions. But now, I am free from identifying myself with the external manifestations of trauma and pain. I know who I truly am.

As you become freer, you are less attached to your behaviours, thoughts and habits. Instead, you can acknowledge and observe them and have the tools to release them. You understand where they come from and why they are there, but you know they are not a part of your identity. Your true identity is beloved, free and a creation of a whole new person filled with love beyond your wildest imagination. You can walk in freedom, and visualisation is a great tool to help you. Your imagination is a beautiful gift from God, and you can use it to find joy in books, stories and adventures. Your imagination can also help you activate your faith. Sadly, many people speak about faith in a language of fear, and they teach us to be afraid of everything. But this takes away from the vastness of God, in my opinion. We are created in His image, so we have an imagination for a reason. This imagination can be used for anything in life, whether it be negative or positive. Using our imagination for love and faith is powerful. We can imagine the things we have been promised and the things we are hopeful for on the screen of our minds. For example, if I say, "See yourself free", you can picture in your head what a woman who is free from pain and trauma looks like and how she lives. This can inform our thanksgiving and help us walk by faith, not physical sight. Suppose we focus only on what we naturally see now. In that case, we might feel trapped because our physical reality won't look perfect. Having faith can seem a bit whimsical or even delusional to some. It requires reaching beyond what we can touch and see and opening up to the possibility of a bigger truth. This concept can be applied to your journey towards personal freedom, healing and renewal. By having faith in the truth of who you are rather than the person you have become due to past experiences and environments, you can move forward with confidence and purpose. There is a place of peace, love, freedom and growth that you may not have seen yet, but you will experience it in your day-to-day life. The rescue has already happened, and all your wounds and pains have been accounted for and carried on your behalf. The road to experiencing this place is a journey into more profound love. We must take this journey into ourselves. Take the journey with God. Accepting this love helps us discover our preciousness and value. You are here on purpose, and your presence in the earth is not an accident. You are here by design. So, as you move forward in freedom daily, remember that the journey is towards love and God – whether that be on a self-healing journey with the support of things you learn through reading and in prayer with the Holy Spirit, in seeking a professional therapist or counsellor to walk alongside you, or in a trusted community of people you love. Whatever path of discovery you choose, the desire and will of God for you is wholeness, freedom, love and truth in the inward parts; to be no longer bound by the words and actions of others or even your own.

Dream, hope and be curious about life and yourself. Don't be afraid to change and embrace the changes that come your way. It's OK if you felt differently about something last month, as you can always explore it further and discover new things. Keep evolving and remember that life is a journey filled with twists and turns and through it all, you are loved!

Reflection

Statement to Ponder:

When you say to yourself that you are no longer bound but free, you are not lying or deceiving yourself. That statement is saying that you accept the gift of life, the gift of love, that has been freely given to you, and you choose to take that journey, to walk into ever-increasing depths of love in an unveiling of your true identity.

Big Breath

I am loved and free. I accept the gift of beloved identity in Christ, as well as freedom, wholeness, healing, peace, and grace. Today, I'll take another step into a deeper depth of love for myself and others. I give thanks that I grow in greater understanding of my identity as I look into the face of the Love that created me.

Other Resources

Books for Further Reading

Donald Miller. 2003 (Blue Like Jazz)
NT USA: Thomas Nelson Publishers

Dr Nicole LePera. 2021 (How To Do The Work).
London: Orion Books UK

Betsy de Thierry. 2018 (The Simple Guide To Understanding Shame in Children).
London: Jessica Kingsley Publishers.

Charles Slagle.1989 (From the Father's Heart).
PA.USA: Destiny Image Publishers

The book below covers very in-depth case studies on trauma. It may not be suitable for everyone.

Bessel Van Der Kolk 2014 (The Body Keeps The Score: Mind Brain and Body in the Transformation of Trauma).
London: Penguin Random House UK

Counselling Services

Mind

https://www.mind.org.uk/information-support/drugs-and-treatments/talking-therapy-and-counselling/how-to-find-a-therapist/

The Black, African and Asian Therapy Network
www.baatn.org.uk

Association of Christian Counselling.
https://www.acc-uk.org

The Women and Girls Network
https://www.wgn.org.uk/our-services/counselling-and-therapeutic-support

The British Association for Counselling and Therapy
https://www.BACP.co.uk

NHS talking therapies
www.nhs.uk/conditions/stress-anxiety-depression/-benefits-of-talking-therapy/

About the Author

Tracey-Jane Campbell is a singer, speaker and founder of "The Outlet House Safe Space for Women." She is a Spurgeon's College graduate, with a bachelor's degree in theological studies. Tracey is passionate about people and their stories. Her own trauma journey inspires her to support others to heal and find freedom.

Notes

[1] Riggio, R.E. 2012. 'There's Magic in Your Smile: How Smiling Affects Your Brain.' Psychology Today. [Online]. Available at: https://www.psychologytoday.com/za/blog/cutting-edge-leadership/201206/there-s-magic-in-your-smile#:~:text=A%20study%20published%20in%20the%20journal%20Neuropsychologia%20reported,view%20a%20person%20smiling%2C%20you%20actually%20feel%20rewarded.

[2] Note that this ideal should be set in the right cultural context, a well-to-do woman would have had help in the form of servants, think Downton Abbey. This gives a clearer understanding that this woman is managing by giving directions to the household workers rather than carrying out all of the tasks herself which is often how the text has been delivered to modern women.

[3] Ferber, S.G.; Feldman, R & Makhoul, I.R. 2010. 'The Development of Maternal Touch Across the First Year of Life.' *Early Human*

About PublishU

PublishU is transforming the world of publishing.

PublishU has developed a new and unique approach to publishing books, offering a three-step guided journey to becoming a globally published author!

We enable hundreds of people a year to write their book within 100-days, publish their book in 100-days and launch their book over 100-days to impact tens of thousands of people worldwide.

The journey is transformative, one author said,

"I never thought I would be able to write a book, let alone in 100 days… now I'm asking myself what else have I told myself that can't be done that actually can?'"

To find out more visit
www.PublishU.com

Printed in Great Britain
by Amazon